T0157434

PLEDGING ALLEGIANCE

PLEDGING ALLEGIANCE

On the Road to Americanization

LEIF BILEN

PLEDGING ALLEGIANCE
ON THE ROAD TO AMERICANIZATION

iUniverse books may be ordered through booksellers or by contacting:

iUniverse
1663 Liberty Drive
Bloomington, IN 47403
www.iuniverse.com
1-800-Authors (1-800-288-4677)

ISBN: 978-1-4917-6653-8 (sc)
ISBN: 978-1-4917-6654-5 (e)

Print information available on the last page.

iUniverse rev. date: 05/08/2015

Contents

PART THREE
Some Adjustment Needed

PART FOUR
Trying to Obey the Lord

PART FIVE
Exercising Personal Options

PART SIX
Final Reflections

Acknowledgements

There are many people who have played a part in ensuring that this book is finally in print. During the last several years, my wife Bonnie has encouraged me to complete what she has referred to as my legacy writing. She thinks that as a naturalized citizen I have a unique perspective to share with grandkids as well as other readers. I am glad she kept reminding me of this, even when a round of golf seemed more appealing. Thank you, Bonnie.

Because some of the content dates back 30 years, I have no doubt forgotten some of the input I received when sharing a few of the early reflections on life that eventually made their way into this book. If you are one of those anonymous folks, please accept my thanks.

Over the last several years, it has been my privilege to meet with dear friends in the Colorado group of the Plot and Blot literary society, and I want to thank Alan Scholes, Gary Stanley and Kirsten Wilson for letting me be part of the group. Their input and wise counsel have encouraged me and kept me going.

I want to thank John Vahlenkamp, managing editor of the *Longmont TIMES-CALL*, for allowing me to include several of the columns I have written for the paper, starting in 2006.

Valuable input from my friend Paul Baker meant a lot to me during the final stages of the project. Many thanks, Paul.

All along, my good friend Jerry Guibor has helped with proof-reading, editing, cover design and the inclusion of pictures as well professional counsel on putting all the various parts together. I doubt if this project would ever have been finished without his help. Thank you, Jerry.

Introduction

As I traveled to my mother's funeral back in Sweden in 1999, I realized that my role had changed drastically. I was now the older generation and the guardian of my parents' legacy. The fact that I am an only child makes this responsibility even more poignant.

I reflected on these things as I met friends and relatives at the funeral, some of whom I had not seen for more than 25 years. Most of them lived only a short distance from where they were born. I, on the other hand, had left my "home port" and tied up for longer or shorter periods in several places on another continent. My relatives find much of their sense of belonging in their surroundings and familiar places. Having lived in eight different homes in four states in America and two countries since my wife and I were married, my sense of belonging is somewhat less geographically based.

I will describe some of the formative events and adventures that have brought me to retired life in Colorado and near the foothills of the Rocky Mountains. There have been many changes and surprising turns on this journey of life. But some things have not changed: my beliefs and values based on my Christian worldview.

In addition, there will be some musings written down over several decades, things that made me laugh when I needed a break from work and responsibility. Others are reflections to show my perspective on life and how it has changed over the years. These are not necessarily in chronological order – rather they have been inserted where they fit the theme of the section. Many of these chapters deal with experiences while driving across the country. Yes, I love the open road, and many of my conclusions of what makes this country great have come as a result of what I have observed and the people I have encountered in the heartland, often called flyover country. This "mental filing" has taken place behind the wheel or in hotel rooms of varying quality.

Overall, I have tried to keep a rather informal tone, even when dealing with serious matters – a kind of fireside chat with family and friends. The appendix contains some of the columns I have written for the local paper, the *Longmont TIMES-CALL*, over the past eight years. They deal with things that matter to me and, I hope, many of my readers.

Leif Bilen
April 2015

PART ONE

My Swedish Heritage

1

A Surprising Turn of Events

If you do not expect the unexpected
You will not find it.
Heraclitus

My earliest childhood memory is sitting in my mother's lap in an air-raid shelter in the basement of our apartment building. I was probably about 3 years old. Sirens had sounded all over the city of Göteborg (Gothenburg), and everyone in the building had descended to safety. These shelters with their massive steel doors and thick concrete walls were a common feature in most apartment houses.

World War II had not yet touched Sweden, but German airplanes often came pretty close to our borders, and an attack appeared likely, considering what had happened to our neighbors, Norway and Denmark. As a toddler, I had no idea what was going on, but I later learned more about this time and what my folks went through.

My folks experienced some tough times. We had to move three times before I started school and lived in one small apartment for one month or so. My dad became a policeman, sort of as a last resort, when jobs in his field, plumbing and heating design, were hard to find.

I remember crying when Dad told me the war was over, because I realized I would lose some of my playmates who were in our community with their parents as refugees from Norway. My folks, of course, had a different perspective, realizing that things would get better – no more air raids or food rationing. I had observed my mother presenting rationing coupons when buying certain food items, thinking it was just normal procedure. I am sure Mom and Dad had to go without certain things, making sure I was well-nourished.

At that time, I was only vaguely aware of the country that has become my home and has accepted me as a citizen. I had some toys, for example, a tiny wind-up car, a Schucomobile, which had a label saying that it was made in the U.S. zone of West Germany. I also had an uncle who worked for the Swedish American Line as a purser on a large passenger ship, and he often brought some presents from America. I remember staring in amazement at a can of Del Monte pineapples. This kind of tropical fruit was almost unheard of at that time in our circle of friends.

Eventually, I learned more about this great country across the ocean and the key role it had played in bringing the war to an end. My father's aunt had emigrated years earlier and had come for a visit. We were awed by her stories. For an only child in elementary school, everything seemed fascinating but unrealistic.

Gradually, I became more aware of the United States. Our teacher told us about "this remarkable country" and tried to make us understand that over there even average people could afford to own a car, for example. To us kids, it sounded almost mythological. We would often hang out around and old Nash owned by the local grocer, practically the only car in the neighborhood, hoping Mr. Sellgren would take one of us along to deliver groceries. As things settled down after the war, more and more cars showed up on the local streets, but they were usually driven by visitors from a more elegant part of town. The ones from the United States we affectionately called "dollar grins," referring to all the fancy chrome in the front that made them look as if they were laughing at us.

The ball-point pen was quite a sensation when it arrived as another reminder of how far ahead America was. In school I had tried, with moderate success, to carefully dip my pen into an ink well, but always having some blotting paper available. My handwriting still leaves a lot to be desired. Fortunately, it didn't take too long before many of us could afford a ball-point pen.

The arrival of Coca-Cola a few years after the war created a bit of confusion in some circles. People in our church were not sure what all the ingredients were, and there was a debate whether a person of faith should really drink this American sensation. Eventually, it was settled, and I came to like the stuff, although the bottles seemed to hold less than what I could get in the old Swedish soft drinks.

My exposure to America was augmented by the books I read. *The Last of the Mohicans* and *The Deerslayer,* along with characters like Hopalong Cassidy and Kit Carson, gave me a sense of America, although there was quite a time warp between that and my geography lessons in school.

Having lived over here more than half my life and pledged allegiance to the "Big Country in the West," I have experienced things that seemed impossible as I was growing up, and I am as surprised as anybody. Stay with me and I'll try to sort it all out.

2

Evald and Gerda

It is not good to have too much liberty.
It is not good to have all one wants.

Blaise Pascal

During a two-week trip to Alberta, Canada, with our Winnebago RV, I always preferred to stop for the night at facilities that offered full hook-ups: water, electricity and a sewer connection. I was not ashamed of my preference, but my grandparents would no doubt have wondered how their first grandchild could have become so spoiled. Their house, where I spent a lot of time as a kid, didn't have the luxury of full hook-ups.

They did enjoy electricity on dark winter nights, and the outhouse was pretty nice, but the water was carried in a bucket from a well about 100 meters from the house. My grandpa, Evald, had dug the well himself. He always made sure there was a full bucket of fresh water on the kitchen counter, before he went to work, although I am sure grandma, Gerda, whom I called *Mormor* (mother's mother), could have managed to fetch one herself.

Something that made staying with Grandma and Grandpa extra special for a city boy were the small farms near their little village, Benareby. The closest farmer, Mr. Larsson, was only a few hundred meters from their house. I used to wait at the gate to Grandma's house and join him most mornings as he took his cattle to pasture. I helped him guide his herd, all of three cows, to a field about a mile away.

These were dairy cows, and we bought our milk from Mr. Larsson. I would fetch it in a metal bucket with a lid, once it had been run through a hand-cranked separator.

The Benareby farmers could barely eke out a living by just farming. To make ends meet, many would make wooden barrels for the fishing industry in town. The town of Göteborg had a bustling fish market, creating a great demand for these barrels.

One village resident made a good living as a fish merchant. He would buy his wares at the market in Göteborg and drive around in a little truck with the fish packed in ice, and stop at every house and farm, and sell what he could. Herring, cod and mackerel were popular dinner items along with the ever-present boiled potatoes, often spiced with dill and plenty of butter.

I don't recall whether the telephone or the sewer and septic tank came first. I was in my late teens when my grandparents' little house finally was close to modern standards with sewer and running water. By that time, Grandpa was suffering from asthma, and they had to sell the house and move to a small apartment in town.

The asthma was a result of him spending hours underneath the house with a hammer and chisel. He was making holes in the granite rock the house was built on, getting it ready for dynamite that would blast away parts of the rock to make room for a basement. Granite dust entered his lungs, eventually causing the disease.

It was always exciting for me to watch the blasts every couple of weeks as the project progressed. We would stand at a safe distance, watching and hoping that the house would still be there after each explosion. The final result was a very nice basement, but my grandfather's body was never the same, and they had to give up on their dream house. He spent his final years sitting in a chair in the small apartment coughing and spitting.

It was sad to see this former soccer athlete so debilitated. He lived to see me graduate from high school and said he was proud to know a high school graduate personally. Evidently, I was the first one in the family. I remember him as a diligent and honest factory worker, and

I was fascinated by the fact that he had handled the factory's horses. Horses pulling carts were a common sight in my early childhood before trucks took over.

His suffering ended shortly before his 74th birthday. Grandma Gerda lived for several more years and visited us often. We were living in Sweden while she was still alive. She was delighted when our kids were born, and it was fun to see her with them. Every once in a while, she would become very thoughtful, staring out the window, saying nothing for a long time. Then suddenly she would burst out, "What do you think of the war? Do you think the Germans will win?" She was repeating a phrase from years back. Although Sweden was not directly involved, she lived through two world wars.

Grandma and Grandpa often had to struggle to make ends meet. Their simple home reflected their modesty and satisfaction with simple pleasures. They seemed content with their life together and enjoyed their extended family. It was a privilege to be one of their grandchildren.

3

A Tradition of Faith

In a small house God has His corner; in a big house,
He has to stand in the hall.
Swedish proverb

Dad's heavy breathing as he was carrying me the few blocks from
the bus stop to our home sometimes woke me up. Being only a few
years old, I wasn't really that heavy, but his deliberate gait and steady
pace tended to make me open my eyes. This was the normal routine
in the early years as we returned from some evening church service.

As was the case for all Swedish citizens in those days, my folks
were members of the Lutheran State Church of Sweden. For them,
it was just a formality; another government institution. Arne and
Majken had chosen to be active members of one of the so-called Free
Churches called *Svenska Missionsförbundet*, which is non-state church
and is related to the Evangelical Covenant Church in the States.

People belonging to the various Free Churches in those days
were referred to as "*läsare*," meaning "readers." The term implied
that they read the Bible on their own and took their faith seriously.
My paternal grandparents, Carl and Hulda, were Free Church folks,
and had influenced many of their nine children in the same direction.
Hulda was seldom able to attend the church services herself because
she had to take care of so many kids in various stages of development.

Carl would attend the Sunday services and then relay the message of the sermon to her upon his return.

I never met Carl. He died of a cerebral hemorrhage at the age of 52. I have only a vague memory of Hulda as she was sitting in her hospital bed a few days before she passed away from cancer. I was only a toddler at the time. This does not mean that the two of them did not influence my life. Their personal faith and their integrity were passed down to me via my parents. They certainly taught me the basic principles of their Christian faith, and how they lived and interacted with each other and friends and neighbors also meant a lot.

I also remember enjoying Sunday school, being especially fascinated by the visual aid of the day: a flannel-covered board where the teacher would put cutout figures of different Bible characters while telling a Bible story. I am told that I once returned from Sunday school and quickly devoured my lunch and asked for more food. When asked the reason for my sudden ravenous appetite, I told mother we could expect seven years of famine. The teacher had done a great job dramatizing the lesson, but I had taken it too literally.

Most of my playmates were not Free Church kids. This was not a big deal for me, but sometimes it meant that I was not allowed to participate in everything they did. In those days, our church was somewhat strict when it came to certain kinds of entertainment. Going to the movies was not considered appropriate. Some of us were trying to come to terms with the fact that we were allowed to watch slide shows in church but not go to the movies. Of course, the slide shows were usually presentations by some missionary to Africa, who was home for a visit. We came up with a rather sarcastic ditty showing how we felt: "Sinful and silly is Buffalo Bill. Sin disappears when the picture is still." This did not go over well with the older generation, although my dad chuckled a bit. In a way, it helped us cope.

The first movie I remember seeing was, believe it or not, shown in church after all. It was a documentary about how sardines are processed and canned. We all thought it was very disgusting. Over time, things have changed, and today's generation of Free Church kids would not recognize any of these tendencies.

The church ran a program for boys, which was a version of the Boy Scouts. We had a lot of fun and learned many useful things at the weekly meetings. The many camping outings were also a big factor for me as an only child, getting to hang out with my peers.

When I was about 12 years old, I started to attend the youth group meetings, which also included girls. During one of the summer camps with this group, I accepted Christ as my personal savior, and I have tried to stay close to Him for the rest of my life. The tradition of faith in my home had laid the foundation, but I still had to make a personal choice and commitment.

My own knowledge of what the Bible teaches originated with the stories my folks read to me and what I learned in Sunday school, as well as attending church services with my parents. Then of course, we learned about Christianity in the public school system. Every year, we took a class called *Kristendom* (Christianity), later renamed *Religion* (same word in English). We even had to learn certain hymns by heart. I am afraid it sometimes made us think that the Bible was just another school book.

Our denomination also offered what was referred to as *Bibelskolan* (Bible school) to young teenagers one night a week for two semesters. There we went more deeply into the Bible message than we did at school. The state Lutheran church did the same with its confirmation classes for the same age group. This was almost seen as a rite of passage for young Swedes in those days, and many parents without a strong personal faith would send their kids to these classes.

Sweden has certainly changed a lot since the '40s and '50s. It has become very secular, similar to many other European countries. People with a strong personal faith are a small minority today, but without knowing it, the society still benefits from the foundation laid by earlier generations with a greater reliance on God and the Bible.

4

Gaining Increased Independence

A ship in the harbor is safe –
but that is not what ships are for.
John A. Shield

Majken and Arne's firstborn was a son who entered the world on a cold February day during the early part of World War II. Filled with joy, they brought him home to their small apartment, which was not far from where Majken's folks lived. While Arne worked hard to make ends meet, the little boy was doted on by his mom and grandma, Gerda. He was her first grandchild.

The proud parents were planning a large family, but that was not to be. Although Majken's next pregnancy resulted in a precious baby girl, Vera, she lived for only 40 minutes. Further, after being in labor for 36 hours, Majken was unable to walk and had to remain in the hospital for three weeks. When she was finally able to return home, she needed to use two canes to get around for about three months. They were devastated but kept trying and praying. After two miscarriages, they realized that their little boy would be an only child.

In Sweden in those days, little was known about the problems caused by the Rh factor after the first pregnancy. In a different era, the other babies may have been saved.

Because her son was the only one who survived, Majken tended to look at him as the perfect child. People who look at me now, know that isn't true, and it was sometimes hard to live up to Mother Majken's expectations.

As I said, the church we attended had a touch of legalism. This was not necessarily expressed in its doctrine, but that is how it felt for the younger generation in view of the kind of behavior that was expected of us. This added to the challenge of trying to be the perfect child. So did the fact that my dad was a policeman, and the expectation was that his son would live up to certain standards and not disgrace the family or his profession.

When I was learning to ride a bike, Dad drew me a map showing the streets I was allowed to use. His intentions were no doubt to ensure my safety, but it meant I couldn't go very far, which was probably just as well, because it was my mom's rather heavy and clumsy bike. When I finally got my own bike, a used one, after a thorough investigation that the seller had not stolen the bike, some of the restrictions were lifted. I remember standing there in the bike repair shop holding my breath until Dad had finished talking to his colleagues in the office dealing with stolen bikes. Children's bikes were a rare commodity at the end of WWII.

Soon thereafter, I had a rather serious accident racing across an intersection with some friends. I was struck by a car and ended up missing the last few weeks of second grade. I still have scar on my right leg, which was punctured by the handlebars. If the earlier restrictions hadn't taught me enough, the injury and its consequences certainly made me more careful.

Eventually, I got what in Swedish was called a *moped*; essentially a bike with a small engine. You were allowed to drive it without a license once you turned 15, and those of us who were lucky enough to get one of those dream machines thought we had come of age and owned the streets. This was despite the fact that the two-cycle engine delivered less than 1 horsepower and top speed was about 20 mph, but boy did it sound powerful. Our family did not own a car at this time, so I ended up putting a lot of miles on it driving it back and forth to school and to our summer home about 10 miles from town. I felt very privileged compared with some of my classmates.

It was probably not a total surprise to Majken that I wasn't perfect, but in some ways I had probably showed both my parents that they could trust me more and more as I got a little older. They enrolled me in a school in downtown Göteborg, although it was a bit farther away. After a few years, they even encouraged me to apply for an exchange student scholarship to attend high school in the United States.

That meant a lot of changes. The mode of transportation was only one of these changes. One of my classmates had a brand-new 1957 Plymouth convertible and took me for a ride. I don't remember whether I even told him about my *moped*. The whole thing was surreal. Read more about the experience that changed my life in the next few pages, initially posted on my daughter Tina's blog, *Life Is Good*, in 2013.

5

The Swede and the Nutritionist

"Do you have indoor plumbing in Sweden?"

"What sort of clothes do you wear over there?"

"Are there many polar bears where you live?"

Those were some of the questions I got from my fellow students at Montgomery Blair High School in Silver Spring, Maryland, as they tried to get to know their new exchange student.

This was during Eisenhower's second term, about half a year before the Soviets launched the first *Sputnik*. The Internet and social media had not yet transformed communications to give us a better awareness of what goes on in other countries around the world. I probably had similar illusions about this country.

I had read *The Last of the Mohicans*, and I had tasted that curious soft drink called Coca-Cola. Then in school, I learned a bit more about the "Big Country in the West," and the more I learned the more interested I became.

When the opportunity for a year's scholarship to an American high school presented itself, there was hardly any hesitation. I applied, and after a few months, a letter advised me I was one of the fortunate ones. I was told I would be going to Silver Spring. "Man, this is going to be great. How can I be so blessed?"

I soon found out that my host family had four children and a maid living with them. The father in the family was an eye doctor. "How am I going to fit in over there?" I was an only child and my dad was a cop, who had to do a lot of moonlighting to make ends meet.

Later, I learned that this was a back-up plan, because the first host, a pastor's family in the same town, had backed out at the last minute. Now I realize how different my life would have been if this change had not taken place.

I was excited and nervous when I prepared to leave my familiar surroundings. As I started to receive letters from members of my new family, I began to calm down. They seemed so nice and genuine. I would be hanging out with a "brother" my age, and his letters were very reassuring.

One letter from his 15-year-old little sister, Bonnie, puzzled me though. She told me it would be nice if I could bring along some Swedish dishes. I didn't quite panic, but I started to wonder. "How are they going to fit in my suitcase? What if they break in transit?" After consulting a dictionary or two, I eventually figured out that she was talking about Swedish recipes, and had I known then what I know today, I would have made sure they didn't lack nutrition.

6

Another Culture

When the *Arosa Sky* of the Holland America Line docked in New York City on August 13, 1957, I was recovering from the Asian flu. I was one of several hundred high school students who had crossed the Atlantic together. Many of us had spent a few days in bed with high fevers and other symptoms. I was not allowed to disembark until local health officials had checked me out and cleared me for entrance into this country: not the greatest start for a year abroad, but it added to the adventure.

From New York City, we headed to our final destinations. Along with several others, I was on a chartered Greyhound bus heading to the Washington, D.C., area. As the bus made its way to the Lincoln Tunnel, I noticed the colorful yellow taxicabs that seemed to be all over the place. Back home, all taxis were black, and the drivers wore black uniforms. "No, this is not going to be a drab and boring country."

A Howard Johnson restaurant with its bright orange roof and iconic architecture caught my eye shortly after entering New Jersey. "Wow, I guess I am not in Europe anymore." It was not the only one along the road. They were all over the place back then. In 2012, there were only two of them left: one in Maine and the other one in New York state. Yes, America's tastes have changed, and in more areas than food, for that matter.

My host family welcomed me with open arms and quickly made me feel at home. During the few weeks before the fall semester, I was able to adjust to several things, although they didn't really come as a huge surprise: a big family, a big house, a big yard, a big church, big cars and so on.

Other curiosities intrigued me. One morning when I walked into the kitchen, there was a man looking into the refrigerator. Then, he walked out the back door and returned with some milk, eggs and butter. The milkman had free access to the house, and it was up to him to determine what the household needed until his next visit. I was used to running to the store for my mother when we were out of something.

Another thing that told me a lot about what kind of neighborhood we were living in was the fact that nobody seemed to worry about locking their cars while parked in the driveway.

I guess the real culture shock came when I started school. I had attended a medium-sized downtown high school for boys. Here I was in a large coed high school on a sprawling campus with huge parking lots for the students who drove their own cars to school, which included Bob, my host brother, who drove me, Bonnie and two other girls. We also had our own stadium for football and other sports. I got used to it faster than I had expected and enjoyed it a lot.

I knew I would probably lose a year of school after returning to Sweden, so I signed up for some unique classes not available back home: driver education (in a 1957 Chevy), public speaking and typing. Although I was a senior, I took 11th-grade English and history, because they dealt with American literature and history. Because Bonnie was a year ahead of her peers, we ended up taking those classes together, and from time to time we helped each other with homework.

Other than that, I stuck with the program and hung out with brother Bob and that included both of us playing on the soccer team. However, there was little doubt that Bonnie was rather cute and pleasant.

7

Now What?

My American exchange adventure went by very quickly. On the way back across the Atlantic, I reconnected with the other students, and we compared notes. Our dress code had changed among other things, and when I greeted my folks, I had a new haircut: a crew cut.

The American "dishes" I brought home were not all that nutritious, but hamburgers, french fries and banana splits tasted awfully good. Please don't tell the "Nutritionist" – our oldest daughter Tina's nickname for my wife.

My American year was a wonderful experience, and although it put me a year behind in the rather stringent academic high school I came home to, I never regretted it. I had two more years before graduation and then mandatory military service in Sweden, before starting my university studies.

"Will I see anyone in my American family ever again?" The answer to that question came rather quickly. Brother Bob came to visit over the summer of 1959, and we toured Europe together: two 19-year-old fellows in a Volvo, where the seats reclined enough to be able to sleep in some semblance of comfort.

I introduced him to most of my friends, many of them girls, wouldn't you know? I am sure we exchanged a word or two about his sister, Bonnie. Although I dated some Swedish girls, during high school and Army days, I wasn't able to put his younger sister out of my mind.

I had a few months after being discharged from the Army before the start of my first semester at the university. I decided to "visit my American family" as I described it to them in my letters. Bonnie's father suspected there was more to it, and I admit he was right.

During that summer, Bonnie and I realized that we were not just foreign exchange brother and sister any more. There was a lot of mutual respect, but also some caution flags: How is this going to work, two continents, different cultures, etc.?

The following summer Bonnie visited Sweden, and the land of the Vikings didn't scare her too much. As she went back to New York to finish nursing school, we agreed to stay in touch, but there was no restriction on dating others. If it were God's plan for us to spend our lives together, it would surely become clear to us.

The only way to stay in touch was via airmail letters, and there were lots of them. After finishing half of my university credits, I had had enough of letter-writing and decided to take some time off and move to New York for a while and leave the rest to the Lord.

Eight months later, we were married. I had a job at Chase Manhattan Bank, while she finished her B.S. degree in nursing. We moved to Sweden for me to finish school, and I promised: "If you don't like it, we can move back to the States."

We stayed for 10 years, and I had a promising teaching career in the public school system as well as some work at the local teacher institute. I also had the privilege of working with my teaching mentor, publishing several books for kids to learn English.

In 1974, I took a sabbatical so that our family, which now included three kids, could spend a year in America. That didn't work out as planned; we are still here, and I eventually became a U.S. citizen. After all, Grandpa shouldn't be the only foreigner in the family.

None of this was planned in 1974, and I have found out that one's life's path is full of small course adjustments. When we stay close to God and listen to his voice, he directs our path, and sometimes these adjustments eventually lead to major changes. In my case, it was a change from teaching to a corporate career with Volvo, which turned out to be a nice ride (pun intended). People wonder these days what happened to that handsome, young Swedish foreign exchange student Bonnie married, and so do I at times. I am an elderly U.S. senior living with my prairie home companion at the foot of the Rockies.

The two of us are very different, and that has in some ways contributed to success in our marriage. Neither of us is perfect, but we are perfect for each other fitting together like two pieces in a puzzle.

PART TWO

Mysteries of Immigration

8

I'm An Owner (1992)

One time when I returned from Sweden, the re-entry process was unusually slow. There we stood, the huddled masses, at least 300 of us, waiting for two passport control officers to check us through. A sign instructed us to wait behind the white line "until we were called." That phrase sounded almost biblical. I stood there watching people approach the officer with a certain amount of trepidation to find out whether we were not only called, but also chosen. Some were not. They were taken to a holding booth with glass walls. After a while, half a dozen people were sitting there nervously awaiting a government decision. They were still there looking dejected and rejected an hour later, when I was finally cleared. Yes, they did let me back into the country.

While all this was going on, U.S. citizens passed quickly through special checkpoints with hardly any wait at all. I remember thinking, "Hey, I'm a homeowner. Let me go through the quick line." You see, even though there is a big mortgage on my piece of America, I do feel as if I belong. I suppose, until the mortgage is paid off, I cannot really lay any claims to the quick line.

Shortly after this episode, I started to look into how to become a citizen, not only because of the immigration process at the airport, of course. I did have other, more valid reasons. However, I discovered that I needed to produce a copy of my driving record to apply for citizenship. I wondered what two speeding tickets in the last three years would do to my chances. It would be ironic if a couple of speeding tickets would keep me in the slow lane at immigration.

But let me tell you about my piece of America. It is 9,716 square feet of northern Virginia clay. We have a comfortable, fairly modest house. The house sits right in the middle of an ecological battlefield. It is the battle between the Virginia clay and Scott's four-step fertilizer program. The builder was evidently of the opinion that topsoil is not vital to establishing a lawn. So far the battle has raged for three years with no clear winner.

I have a covenant relationship with my neighbors. We are all members of the CABIN BRANCH FOREST HOMEOWNERS ASSOCIATION, INC. This means that on my piece of the land of liberty, I am not really free to do as I please because "the real estate is subject to certain covenants, restrictions, reservations, easements, servitudes, and charges, all of which are more particularly hereinafter set forth." In a 60-page document, I might add.

"No lot shall be used for transient or hotel purposes." I think our daughter violated this covenant during spring break. "A reasonable number of roommates is permitted." I wonder whether we can make exceptions for in-laws.

I find that I must avoid junk or derelict vehicles. If I own one, I must not let my neighbors see it. Close that garage door. I am not sure my neighbors appreciate the 1959 Volvo I keep and cherish. I do not consider it junk, but the county only charges a token property tax of $4.20. I will ensure it does not exhibit any derelict tendencies.

I may not keep, board or raise "animals, livestock, poultry, or reptiles." Our dog Salli is permitted only if we qualify her as an "orderly domestic pet." However, should she create any "unreasonable disturbance or noise," she may be permanently removed from the property.

"No offensive trade or activity shall be carried on . . . within any dwelling." This I need to think about. Cleaning up after the dog is something I find rather offensive, but then again it would probably be more offensive not to do it.

I can't burn trash. I need written approval for a TV antenna. I must keep the trash can out of public view, except on Tuesdays and Fridays. Tents, shacks and barns are no-nos. After 60 pages of this stuff, you get dizzy. All I can hope is that my neighbors will love me and my dog and my lawn the way we do. I know the Lord does.

9
Red Tape (1997)

The immigration issue had caught up with me again. Still living here on a green card, I was supposed to notify the INS of any change of address. After moving to Virginia, I called them. I actually got through to a real, live person. I was almost too astonished to speak.

"Immigration!"

"Hi, I am a registered alien with a green card. I have moved, and I understand I have to give you my new address."

"You need to use a special form."

"I'm sorry, but I don't have one."

"We'll send you one. What's your address?"

I gave them my new address, which the person carefully wrote down and read back to me.

I said, "Now that you have my address, maybe this is enough?"

"No, you still have to use the form."

A few days later, an official brown envelope arrived with my name and address neatly on the front. Inside was an address form, which I filled out and sent back to them so they could record it one more time. I was amused as well as a little irritated, but most of all I was relieved to be legal again.

Bureaucracy can be humiliating as well as a little irritating. Seldom do I feel as ignorant as when I try to register a new or used car. This happens with some regularity. I have bought various used cars for the kids, and the employee lease car we used to get every two years had to be titled to my employer, but registered to my home address.

I have never been to the Department of Motor Vehicles without having to stand in line with about 15 other people running similar errands. I have been successful on the first try only once. All other times, I have been sent home for remedial work. Registering the lease car is the worst assignment. Last time, it took three trips through the 15-person line. First, I did not have my employer's federal tax number handy. Then, it was discovered that the power of attorney I had was for titling the car only. I needed to register it as well.

As I said, it is a humbling experience to fail DMV 101, particularly for an auto executive. Plus, I pay taxes for this privilege.

When I moved to Colorado in 1997, I was determined to get it right the first time. After all, I was going only to register a truck I already owned with clear title. The new car I was buying from my now former employer had not arrived. The trouble was, they would not accept my Virginia title and registration without a vehicle identification number verification. VIN verifications are done at the facilities that perform emission tests. Don't ask me why. Further, only the supervisors, evidently, are authorized to verify VINs. The verification of the number was done without looking closely at the truck itself. The man's only interest in looking at my truck was determining its color, which went something like this.

"This truck is blue, right?"

"Sir, I believe Ford refers to it as deep forest green."

"Nah, looks blue to me."

I did not challenge his impression of the color. I knew better. I would have lost that argument. Besides, I have learned the hard way never to ruffle the feathers of an official connected with the DMV.

10

Life With the Green Card (2002)

Here is your green card," the embassy official said. "I know it is blue, but it used to be green, so we still call it the green card." The process was finally over. I was allowed to enter this bastion of freedom and private enterprise as a registered alien. That title sounded almost as good as my wife's title. She is a registered nurse. To gain this status, I had promised not to overthrow the government or become a burden to society. I had sworn that I did not belong to the Communist Party. They had checked me over and determined that I did not have any deadly or contagious disease. I don't know whether my rosy cheeks helped any, but I was glad that my cold had finally cleared up. My wife, as an American citizen, had promised in writing that she would personally guarantee my upkeep. That probably clinched it. By the strength of her birthright, they were assured that precious tax dollars would not be spent on a freeloader from a country whose basic fabric is a strong social safety net.

Well, here I am years later. I had promised Richard Nixon, or at least his man in Stockholm, that I would not cheat the government, or (in Nixon's own words) that I was not a crook. If I can be pardoned for some speeding tickets and one other moving violation, I am pleased to say that I have kept my word.

My wife's written promise of economic support has never really been tested. We have been able to pay for the groceries. I think we are a good team. She went back to work as a nurse to allow us to put the kids in a Christian school. I don't know whether you are interested in all this, but I want you to know that your tax dollars are not at work here.

As a registered alien, I really had all the obligations and most of the privileges of a citizen. I am stretching things a bit here, because during the Vietnam War (during an earlier stay), I found out that I was subject to the draft. I did register with the Selective Service System. However, I was not allowed to drive a New York City bus or subway train. Not that I really wanted to, but it struck me as odd that you would trust someone with a gun to defend the country, but that same person could not be trusted with a steering wheel. I really did not think I was a security risk. Anyway, Kennedy saw to it that I did not have to go to Vietnam, when he ruled that married men would be chosen last. I am, in fact, grateful to all my presidents. To Eisenhower for receiving all of us exchange students at the White House. I will tell my grandchildren. To Nixon for believing I was not a crook. To Kennedy, as I said, for not making me a Vietnam statistic. (I did not give Johnson much of a chance. We spent most of our time in Sweden while he was in office.) To Ford for being so human and for making me think that I too could learn to play golf. To Carter, bless his heart, for doing away with the obligation to send in my address once a year. I sometimes forgot. The IRS always knew where to find me anyway. To Reagan for stopping runaway inflation, and making us believe in ourselves again. To Bush for a class act showing that he believed that substance is more important than spin control, and for living up to that credo. At the same time, he was such a regular guy. Not only did he play golf, but he also went fishing and took showers with his dog. He also gave me the courage to tell my family that I don't like broccoli. To Clinton for accepting my application for citizenship. I had better stop there. To W for not wavering in doing what he thinks is right. Most of the time I agree with him.

Yes, I did become a naturalized citizen a few years ago. That term "naturalized" sounds so healthy to me, by the way. I can now take part in the political process and even vote for who will be president. My first voting experience was very mundane, though. It was a referendum for a racetrack in Loudon County, Virginia. I voted against the project.

Several years ago, I was driving with a colleague from St. Louis to the Lake of the Ozarks. We were discussing the upcoming presidential election against the backdrop of television debates and endless analyses by the TV pundits. It is easy to overdose on the media circus every four years. Night was falling as we approached Kingdom City. What a glorious name for a small town in a federal republic! As we turned south toward Jefferson City, I saw the lights come on in the farmhouses, and I was struck by one thought. Who cares, really, what the professional political spectators really think? It is the people here in the heartland and elsewhere in the nation who really decide. As we stopped at a Howard Johnson's, a place where the solid citizens like to eat, I was warmed by the sight of the Missouri farmers taking their nourishment on their way back from town. To me at that moment, they personified the American core values as they sat there eating their food with lots of gravy – nothing exotic, no quiche, not too crunchy, no secret recipes. Having been approved for citizenship not too long before, I feel more of a sense of belonging, and I am proud when I tell people that I am an American. I just hope I can live up to the ideals I sensed there at Howard Johnson's. I would be pleased, if someone one day would look at me sitting there with a plate of meat loaf and mashed potatoes and gravy, and say to himself, "There goes a solid citizen."

11

Naturalization

I take this obligation freely without any mental
reservation or purpose of evasion; So help me God.
From the Oath of Allegiance

In one sense, naturalization is a prime example of ultimate bureaucracy, but in another and greater sense, it is a beautiful manifestation of what this country is all about. One of the strengths of this great nation has been its willingness to accept immigrants from all corners of this round globe. I am extremely proud to be one of them. Immigration in the second half of the 20th century, by way of jetliners, is perhaps at times less dramatic than it was 100 years ago, when more than a million Swedes immigrated. However, for the individuals concerned, it is no less life-changing, even though the reasons for leaving one's native land may be different. I obviously did not leave Sweden due to any crop failure, as was the case in 1867, 1868 and 1869.

I was very happy for a number of years as a registered alien and, when I finally made the decision to apply for citizenship, it was precipitated by a planned government administrative action. I received a notice that I would have to renew my green card, with an attached suggestion that this might be a good time to become naturalized. The government later changed its mind for sound fiscal reasons. It would have been too expensive to issue new green cards to everybody, and I, for one, never understood what would have been gained by it anyway. When the decision not to go ahead with the new green cards came, I was already in the middle of the naturalization process, and I had decided that I really wanted to become a citizen. After all, we had decided to stay, and our daughters had married and were thinking of starting families. I was at times amused and irritated by the bureaucracy of it all. At other times, I was on an emotional roller coaster caused by the ties, formal and otherwise, that I was severing, as well as by the bonds and allegiances I was going to declare by an oath.

There is an awful lot of paperwork involved in becoming a citizen of this land of liberty. This seems like a bit of a paradox because many people through the years have come here to escape the onerous burdens imposed by many foreign governments. It seemed like a daunting undertaking when I first looked at the forms I had to fill out and read about all the attached documentation that was required. The INS had anticipated this reaction. A "Paperwork Reduction Act Notice" was part of the package. The INS stated that it had tried to create forms and instructions "that are accurate, can be easily understood, and which impose the least possible burden." INS went on to explain that this is difficult because "some immigration laws are very complex." INS also said that "the reporting burden for this collection of information is computed as follows: (1) learning about the law and form, 20 minutes; (2) completing the form, 25 minutes; and (3) assembling and filing the application (includes statutory required interview and travel time, after filing application), 3 hours and 35 minutes, for an estimated average of 4 hours and 20 minutes per response." Although I was planning only one response, I was not reassured, but I went ahead. I was invited to make suggestions for simplifying the form and about the accuracy of the estimate itself. I was informed that the Office of Management and Budget is hard at work on a "Paperwork Reduction Project." I did not want to complain. Who knows? It might have ruined my chances for approval. Just kidding. After becoming a citizen, I have not felt led to get involved in the "Paperwork Reduction Project."

In assembling the documentation, my first problem was that I was unable to find my draft card. I had registered with the Selective Service System back in 1963, but my card was nowhere to be found. I knew I had not burned it. I wasn't a hippie who protested the war, but I thought even losing the card could be a federal crime. Would I face deportation? I went by the office where I had registered in Silver Spring, Maryland. I couldn't find the office. It was gone as well. After calling around, I was told that old registration records were stored somewhere in Illinois. The official I spoke to couldn't understand why an old guy like me was interested in a draft card from the '60s, but he obliged me with a form to forward the request to Illinois. The form did not ask for the reason for the request, but it did require my signature or as an alternative, "proof of death." I mailed it on March 23, 1993, with the signature, that is, and heard nothing back for a long time. I tried reaching someone on the phone, but got only recorded announcements. Living in the Washington, D.C., area, I was hard-pressed to understand why we don't have enough government workers to answer the phone. Close to despair, I sent in my naturalization application on May 22, 1993, anyway. I attached an explanation as to why a copy of my draft card was not included. I tried to make it as matter of fact and innocuous as possible. Then I held my breath, for almost two months. Suddenly, in the middle of July, I got a letter from Palatine, Illinois. The operations manager went to great lengths to explain why my medical records had been destroyed, and why he could not tell me the reasons for my classification. I did not care. A copy of my draft card was enclosed. Now I was home free, in the land of the free and the home of the brave.

Scrutinizing the card, I came across some interesting details. I had grown taller since 1963, by one full inch, and Sweden was classified as a "cobelligerent nation." That would have given some of my pacifistic former countrymen pause. One item on the classification record did bother me. It listed me as overage for military service on April 22, 1966. Here I was, 27 years later, still thinking I had a bright future ahead of me, and I was overage already then.

The rest of the application provided less drama for me, but it dug deeply into my past. In fact, it focused more on my past, I thought, than on whatever contributions I might make in the future. It was obviously intended to screen out undesirable elements. The questions did not really offend me, but some of them were very unusual. The first few were of the usual political type that I remembered from the visa applications. I have never been a member of the Communist Party, nor have I been affiliated with the Nazi government of Germany, so I was clear on that score. Other "eligibility factors" included assuring the INS that I had never been a habitual drunkard (I guess occasional boozing would have been OK), nor practiced polygamy. I also had to swear that I had neither been a prostitute nor an illicit trafficker in narcotic drugs or marijuana. Now, I am all in favor of keeping undesirable elements out, but I really wonder how many drug traffickers or prostitutes would acknowledge their sins in writing.

When the government wanted to know what organizations I had belonged to, I tried to be as thorough as my memory would allow. They now knew not only what churches I have been a member of, but it was also a matter of official records that I played in the Montgomery County Adult Soccer League in 1975 and 1976.

It took me a long time to reconstruct my trips abroad. My old passports helped, but listing the reasons for my trips became a tearful experience. Several trips were for business reasons, but as the rest of them progressed from "visit parents" to "father's illness" and "father's funeral," I was reminded of those sad trips. By the way, when I was asked upon my return from my father's funeral in 1990, whether the trip had been for business or pleasure, neither category fit, and I was left speechless.

Several months after submitting my application, I was called to "an examination of my application including the statutory required interview."

I was reasonably confident I would pass scrutiny, even though it included a written citizenship test. I had taken American history as an exchange student and kept up with most of the current news. I did prepare by looking at some articles in an encyclopedia the night before. I guessed at what would be pertinent. Sitting around the room with all the other applicants, however, I got nervous. They seemed to be studying elaborate textbooks prepared especially for this purpose. Some of my college experiences came back to haunt me, such as when the test dealt with issues I had not brushed up on the night before. I am pleased to say I passed the test. I got all the answers right, including the Bill of Rights, Washington, Jefferson and Lincoln. The Supreme Court was in there as well as 1492, and the three branches of government. The 13 stripes on the flag was not really a trick question, but probably the most obscure one.

The interview went well. The only sticking point seemed to be the fact that my wife and I had been married for 30 years at the time. I had to confirm that several times with the interviewer who seemed surprised. I don't know why the INS official had a hard time believing me.

At the naturalization ceremony, I was given an official certificate from the Department of Justice as proof of citizenship along with my personal copy of the Declaration of Independence. These are the outwards signs, however. What sticks in my memory is the ceremony itself. All the formality and bureaucracy culminated in an emotional high on December 17, 1993. Several hundred of us were seated in alphabetical order in a high school auditorium. The various names representing different ethnic origins served as a tangible reminder of the melting pot. I had declined, when asked, whether I wanted to change my name on becoming a citizen. So had most of the others, it seemed.

Nuru Yasin Abeldhayi was first in line, and Senait Tefera Zewde was last. In between, the names ranged from Douglas Kent Allen to Lang Duc Luu, from Leif Arne Bilen to Sumintra Jamiroon Mohanni.

The assistant district director of examinations was the master of ceremonies. The Daughters of the American Revolution were represented; the Oakton High School Orchestra played the National Anthem. Boy Scout Troop 1509 and Cub Scout Pack 1509 presented the colors. We took the oath together "abjuring all allegiance and fidelity to any foreign prince, potentate, state or sovereignty." The archaic language almost obscured the significance of the oath. Although the Selective Service thought I was too old, I did promise to defend the Constitution and laws of the United States of America against all enemies, foreign and domestic. As an approved citizen, this is an obligation I do not take lightly. I hesitate to call citizens by birth non-approved, but it occurs to me that many people live and act as if they could not promise such a thing.

One of the speakers told us that we should proudly call ourselves Americans, but that we also had an obligation to share our ancestral legacy with our children and grandchildren. That, he said, the rich and varied heritage of all Americans, is a strengthening hallmark of this country. It made sense. We filed out into the lobby when the ceremony was over. The lobby was full of people involved in local politics asking us to register to vote.

Since then, I have traveled back to Sweden on business several times. It is nice to return and stand in the U.S. Citizens line with my U.S. Passport. Conversely, it has been odd not to stand in the corresponding line when entering Sweden.

Almost a year later, when I had started to feel established as a citizen, I got a surprise from the INS. In a curious case of governmental inefficiency and administrative foul-up, I got a letter saying INS clerks were processing my application for citizenship and I had been scheduled for an interview. I was puzzled and a little amused. First, they made me a citizen, and then they forgot all about it. I got it straightened out. I wasn't ready for more than one U.S. citizenship at a time.

Clockwise from left: My parents, Arne Bilen and Majken Bengtsson, during their courting days in the late 1930s. A neighbor boy and I play in front of our row apartment house. My parents purchased it in 1943. Our door was the second from the left. I am visiting my maternal grandparents, Evald and Gerda Bengtsson, with my mother, Majken Bilen. My paternal grandmother, Hulda Bilen, holds me in her lap, as my cousin, Ingemar Bilen, sits at her knee.

Above: I couldn't believe it. I had my own bicycle for the first time, and I did not have to ride my mother's heavy, clumsy model. Below left: My mother and I return with a full basket from a productive walk to the grocery store. Below right: I showed an early interest in Volvo cars, like this PV60, which was introduced in 1946.

At left: It's the final day of school for another year, and pupils are making their way home. I pause to have my picture taken. I had completed the second grade and was 9 years old.

At right: I am growing up fast, and I sport a new suit after finishing Bible school. Not too many years in the future, I would be attending high school as an exchange student in America. It was a life-changing experience for me.

PART THREE

Some Adjustment Needed

12

A New Career (1981)

When I went for my interview with Volvo, I was making $8,000 a year at the Union Trust Company of Maryland. I had a wife and three kids. Volvo could be our big break. My most recent job had been as a junior high school teacher in Sweden. My background included a bus company, a trucking company and a plumbing company in Sweden, as well as the Chase Manhattan Bank in the United States. I had co-authored some books. I was still wondering about my chances. Where was my specific auto industry experience?

I parked my 1970 Dodge Coronet station wagon (with four drum brakes and no power assist) and walked into the lobby of the Holiday Inn at US 1 and the Beltway in Maryland. Forty-five minutes later, I thought my lack of automotive experience would be a moot point. Cy Shelton, the man who headed up Volvo's local office, had not shown up.

So much for my big break.

I am glad I hung around, though. The gentleman did eventually show up, along with his wife. They spent considerable time talking with me, although they had another engagement that evening. I am also glad that he thought I could make a contribution to his organization. Whereas I focused on experience, he focused on potential and I was hired. That turned out to be good for me, and I trust also for Volvo.

My first assignment as Owner Relations Representative was a perfect entry into the car business. I had to deal with customers, dealers and support staff in all disciplines immediately. I knew cars, and I loved cars, especially Volvos.

Six-and-a-half years later, I attended Cy's funeral.

I am fortunate to have worked for him, and I learned from him. He was the incarnation of unselfish leadership. He cared enormously for his staff. Having recovered from lung cancer, which was operated on a year or so earlier, he was diagnosed with brain cancer on February 25, 1980. Before learning this, he invited my wife and me to dinner that same evening. It was my 40th birthday. He did not cancel. He and his wife honored me with a wonderful meal at Trader Vic's on 16th Street in Washington, D.C. He mentioned, but did not discuss, his illness.

Cy kept working, although his health deteriorated rapidly. Chemotherapy did not slow him down nor did losing almost all of his eyesight. He just made sure one of us traveled with him.

The way he exercised leadership paid off when we had to assume more responsibility. Although his advice was always available, he seldom told us what to do. He allowed us to make mistakes, but he would not tolerate the same mistake twice. He was a master with words, especially when he did not mince them.

First Baptist Church of Alexandria was filled to capacity for the funeral service. A large number was Volvo people whose lives had been touched by Cy. His Christian faith had been an example to many of us. I was honored to be a pallbearer. The service was both a farewell and a celebration.

Two of us made the trip to Danville, Virginia, the following day for the burial. Cy was from Danville and the South Boston area. Incidentally, Cy had appointed C.G. Hairston of Danville to be the first African-American Volvo dealer in the United States. Cy and C.G. shared in the pride of that fact. Now Cy was to be buried in C.G.'s area of responsibility. My emotions at the gravesite overlooking the lush Dan River Valley are not easy to describe. The pastor said something, though, that has been etched in my memory ever since.

"Some of you standing here are not only saddened by Cy's death. You may also be regretting the fact that you never really thanked Cy for what he did for you. The way to thank and honor Cy is to do for someone what he did for you."

Those words spoke volumes directly to me. Since then, I have tried to express my gratitude to Cy in the way the pastor suggested.

13

Tension or Tenure (1986)

"You had better pack a suit. We may need you to fly back here next week and explain this thing."

Those were the words of my boss over the phone at Volvo headquarters approximately 1,700 miles away. I had called to remind him I had a week's vacation scheduled. "This thing" was an unauthorized temporary relocation of one of our dealers. It had happened without my prior knowledge or approval, but I was the District Manager, and there was an implication that I had taken my eye off the ball. Some were thinking I had screwed up.

The whole situation made me realize how far I had come from the relative serenity and security of academic life. I had left a teaching position with full tenure 12 years earlier in Sweden. I had chosen instead the hard knocks of the automobile business in what is probably the most competitive market in the world.

We did take off for the Grand Tetons and Yellowstone with the kids and my folks, who were visiting from Sweden. My suit was in a garment bag on top of all the vacation gear in the back of the station wagon. As I led the family convoy (we had taken two cars) up Interstate 25 toward Wyoming, I was at peace with the decisions I had made. I felt confident that I would be able to justify to management how the district had handled the matter. Yet I sensed a certain amount of insecurity along with a lot of tension, as I was wondering what kind of connections Continental Airlines might have between Jackson, Wyoming, and Newark, New Jersey.

My recollection is that my folks and my wife and kids enjoyed the vacation. I know they had a grand time spotting moose and elk and other wildlife in Yellowstone. I was too busy looking for phone booths at rest stops and intersections. I was supposed to call in once or twice a day. This was long before we had cell phones. Often I was unsuccessful in trying to reach someone at headquarters. "Not at his desk" or "in a meeting" was the usual response. Then there was the time difference between Mountain and Eastern time zones.

As it turned out, I did not have to fly back, and the whole thing was resolved a few weeks later without a lot of fanfare. I got to keep my job!

As we drove back home across that vast expanse of prairie land, where the deer and the antelope play, I started to think about the differences between my previous career and my new one. Had I made the right choices?

I realized that those choices had placed me in a society where vacation certainly does not appear to be one of the inalienable rights. To a Swede, personal time is sacred. The standard of living equation takes into account the length of your vacation. Many Swedes have a union mentality when it comes to their jobs. My father, who was in the back seat as these thoughts went through my head, was enjoying retired life and a decent pension as a result of social legislation passed decades earlier. Recently, he had been able to count on five weeks of uninterrupted personal time every summer. I was wondering whether I would have five uninterrupted days. Why would I be willing to put up with it? What were the trade-offs?

Well, in my particular case, and it may well be symptomatic of the national differences, the States had allowed me to break away from monotony. A monotonous job with a monotonous pay scale and a certain amount of monotony associated with a homogenous society. I preferred the change of pace, variety and opportunity that my new career in my new country offered. I wouldn't have traded it for five weeks of vacation, ever. I guess most people enjoy a challenge. It is good for your mind and for your body. I probably was kidding myself thinking that the company couldn't do without me for five days. Nobody is that important.

P.S, As it turned out, I had a wonderful career at Volvo Cars of North America, which I touch on in an earlier book titled *They Put Me in Charge And Told Me I Didn't Have a Clue* (AuthorHouse, 2009). For this reason, I will not go into too much detail about the car business at this time, although my time at Volvo certainly influenced my life in many ways.

14

Durability (1987)

I have always liked cars. I especially like old cars. Of course, there is a lot of sentimentality involved. When I was a young teenager, my family could not afford a car, and I looked with envy at automobiles of any kind. Most Swedish kids at the time would have given up a month's allowance for a short ride in some rich relative's "dollar grin," with those big, toothy chrome grilles grinning from fender to fender. Those were the days. The dollar was strong. The American auto industry seemed invincible, and those V8s were indestructible.

When my dad, who was a policeman, was assigned patrol car duty, he took me for a ride in a police car. I thought I had died and gone to heaven.

It was about this time that Volvo introduced the PV444. This was the first Swedish car built with the postwar family in mind, and the thing did not look like a taxicab. Our house happened to be located at the end of the test route that the quality control engineers took when they road-tested those PVs, after they rolled off the assembly line. They would stop by our back yard to fill out a checklist. Invariably, I would strike up a conversation with those drivers. We would discuss the virtues of the PV. Pretty soon, I knew the specs backward and forward, at least at an elementary school level. The PV became the car of my dreams, at least until my father years later brought home an old Ford that he miraculously had been able to afford. But that is another story.

Now my means have changed, but my automotive values have not, and I am part of the automotive industry representing Volvo in the United States. When I decided to buy an old PV and try to restore it, I did so for a variety of reasons. I wanted something to do during my spare time. Not that I have a lot of time on my hands, but I need something to counterbalance job-related stress. There was also a corporate reason. The PV had built our company's reputation over here, and I felt it was a project worthy of my attention. Mostly though, it was going to be an odyssey into automotive nostalgia. That it has been! Struggling with some rusty bolt, I have sometimes thought, "Here I am loosening a bolt that a countryman of mine installed and torqued to the right specs 28 years ago." Thousands of miles away, on a different continent, I am trying to restore the fruit of his labor to its original condition. As he sits there in his rocking chair, waiting for his pension check, wondering whether he ever made a difference, I want to tell him that in Englewood, Colorado, USA, people will turn their heads for years to come, when this indestructible machine rolls down the street, and that the Volvo Corporation is strong thanks to the quality reputation for which this car laid the foundation.

I warned you about nostalgia.

I bought two cars, actually, using the best parts from each one for the restoration. The end product will be a combination of a 1959 and a 1966. Very little had changed between those years, which, as it happens, were the first and the last years the PV544 was manufactured. It had been preceded by my childhood favorite, the PV444.

Pound for pound, my PV would be mostly a '66, but because some of the body parts, particularly the firewall with the serial number, come from the '59, it would be registered as a '59. I had received title of ownership from the previous owner, but the lady at the DMV remarked that the car had a very low VIN (vehicle identification number). I did not think much about it, but decided to check the number on the car anyway. It did not come close to the one on the title. That is when my education in state bureaucracy began.

I am sort of the worrying kind anyway, and all sorts of thoughts started going through my head. Did I have the wrong title or the wrong car? Was it stolen? Was someone going to be able to claim ownership after I had spent months working on this thing? Eventually, of course, sanity prevailed. I had to admit that the likelihood of someone turning up to claim legal rights to this car body that I had rescued from under a heap of trash in Mr. Frothingham's garage was not great. Furthermore, the name Frothingham sounded so trustworthy, as if he had stepped out of a Victorian novel.

Just to be sure, though, I decided to contact the person who had sold him the car, at least according to the incorrect title.

Neither of them had ever worried about the VIN. Neither of them seemed glad to hear from me. Sorry fellow, that's your problem now. They acted as if they wanted to get off the phone as quickly as possible. I had prided myself, when I bought the car, that I had negotiated a good price – a steal, as the saying goes. All of a sudden that sounded ironic to me. Was I after all dealing with stolen property?

I asked the DMV what to do. They gave me two sets of instructions, a yellow sheet to apply for a VIN and a green one to apply for a title correction or a bond title.

"What's a bond title?"

"Well, we want to make sure the car isn't stolen." (There we go again.) "And you will have to purchase a surety bond."

Now the legwork began.

Step one.

A Colorado state law enforcement officer would have to determine which of the two numbers to use. I must admit that Officer Hoff was very friendly and accommodating. He even came to the house to look at the PV in my garage. He seemed impressed. He wrote down the number, filled out two documents and handed them to me to apply for a new title.

Step two.

Request a bond title search at the Colorado Department of Revenue. This required two trips to downtown Denver.

Step three.

Establish a retail value of the vehicle and have it verified by a Volvo dealer on his letterhead. One extra business trip to a local merchant was all it took. He was very accommodating when the district manager (me) showed up with this request.

Step four.

Purchase a surety bond for twice the retail value as shown on the appraisal. Here "my fingers did a lot of walking" before I found someone who was willing to sell me a bond.

Step five.

Write a statement giving information why bonding for ownership is required. Hey, it wasn't my idea.

Step six.

Have above statements notarized.

Step seven.

Go back to the DMV and apply for a new title.

Because I was going out of town and did not want to lose my car (be serious), I did all this very promptly. The lady at the DMV, who had been very helpful, was surprised to see me so soon. I don't know whether it was all worth it. I do know that I had spent hours, driven many miles, paid fees, and taken up a lot of official time to correct a VIN that had probably been incorrect for almost 30 years. All the officials empathized with me saying it was all kind of ridiculous, but it had to be done.

Who made these rules? Whatever happened to the land of liberty?

15

Cross Country (1988)

I am one of Volvo's migrant workers. I guess I did not screw up too badly in Denver. After nine years in various positions in the Washington area, I spent five years running the Denver operations. Headquarters moved me back to Washington and made me manager of one of the largest districts in the country. Now I was back in charge of the district where, once upon a time, I started cutting my automotive teeth.

As I indicated earlier, I had opted for the USA, the automotive industry and Volvo, rather than the relative security and serenity of teaching in Sweden. I like a challenge and seem to thrive on change.

When it comes to challenges and changes, Volvo didn't disappoint me. We took off for Denver, sight unseen, when our oldest daughter was about to enter her senior year in high school. Timing could have been better, but she is a winner and handled it admirably. I think she profited from the experience. The other kids would have had to change schools anyway. We got to Denver when things were booming. We paid a premium for our house, but we liked the area. The following year, the oil industry took it on the nose, but we had fallen in love with the place. It did not really matter, therefore, that the business climate was less than ideal for meeting sales objectives dreamed up by someone 1,700 miles away. We were ready to stay there for the rest of our lives. Or so we thought. When the offer came to take on the job in Washington, my boss also told me that they would be closing the Denver district in about a year. I didn't really have much choice.

We obviously noticed a vast difference between the East Coast and the West. I am not just talking about sea-level vs. mile-high living, but humidity vs. dry air, thick foliage vs. the virtual lack thereof, the Chesapeake Bay vs. the mountains and the prairie. I am also talking about the people, their attitudes and mentality.

There is still a good portion of pioneer spirit to be found out west. Abundant space and open vistas, where you can see forever, seem to have a contagious effect on the mind. People are open to new ideas and seem willing to try various things. I am not talking just about ski bums. I know an engineer from Martin Marietta who opened a sandwich shop. A good friend, who had graduated from the Naval Academy in Annapolis and served in Vietnam as a helicopter pilot, landed in Denver and decided to become a dentist. A hospital administrator at one of the Denver-area hospitals opened one of the best seafood restaurants there. I heard of a lawyer running a kite shop. I don't blame him. Even I got the idea that I could write a book. I'd like to think that the area has had a genuine influence on this immigrant. I don't know though. Maybe it's just the thin air.

People in the East seem to be a bit more set in their professional ways. Please note that I am not talking about the political climate. As you know, that is quite another story.

Anyway, when I got the news from Volvo, I did the sure thing. I moved east again, even though a cinnamon bun franchise seemed intriguing. Moving back was quite a transition for the entire family. In fact, the entire family did not move back. Tina, our oldest, decided to stay in Colorado. She liked the area that much and one of the local boys even more. She ended up teaching school in Berthoud. Linda, our middle child, was at a small college in Minnesota, so there were only three of us moving back. As I worried about selling our house in Denver, even at a loss, I also fought the empty-nest syndrome, while trying to get used to my new job and act coherent in front of my new employees.

Initially, my wife and son stayed in Denver, hoping the house would sell quickly. Although I racked up a lot of bonus miles with United Airlines going back and forth on weekends, it was hard on body and soul. Therefore, we left our house in Denver in the care of our real estate agent and shacked up in a small apartment in Virginia temporarily. Eventually, we moved into a new house in Sterling, Virginia, and our old house in Denver sold. We hadn't had a stream of prospects, but it took only one.

I have been as guilty as anyone in mostly flying over the heartland. I have landed here and there for business purposes, but I had never really driven between Denver and the East Coast. Therefore, my son and I seized the opportunity when we needed to get one of the cars to Virginia. We really did experience the vastness and variety of this continent during our three-day, 1,700-mile trip. We left Denver in bright sunshine and dashed across Kansas on Interstate 70 under similar conditions. We hit Missouri shortly after a storm had put a sheet of ice on the road. Most of it had melted by the time we got there, but the trees were still frosted over. It was beautiful. Illinois and Indiana were cold and cloudy, and Kentucky and West Virginia were beautiful in springtime splendor. We got to Virginia, our new home, late one Saturday night. We could not see the scenery, but the weather was mild and quite promising.

We had traveled through nine different states, met people and experienced things that no air traveler will ever have the privilege of doing. I wish all businessmen like me would have the privilege of breaking away for just a few days to experience the heartland.

There is something reassuring about reattaching yourself to the land, seeing and meeting the people who make their living off the land, sharing a strip of concrete with those 18-wheelers that are piloted by that free-spirited group of pioneers called truckers, eating at places that are not part of some national marketing scheme. There is something basically honest about a place along the highway where the sign simply reads "FOOD." When you drive into the parking lot trying to find a space for your imported sedan among all the large trucks and smaller pickups, you feel as if you are trespassing. You sit down and a wholesome-looking girl from some nearby farm hands you the menu. Her smile tells you the food is going to be good, both for your body and your soul. The food is basic, the portions generous, and the prices moderate. You put the coffee cup to your lips and enjoy the sensation of thick real porcelain. You feel sorry for those people who have to drink their coffee out of a plastic foam cup at some fast-food place. The sight of the farmers and the truckers conversing restores your faith in solid values. You hate to leave after finishing your meal, but as you approach the cash register, you dig deep into your pockets for cash. The whole experience is so solid you would not feel right paying with a credit card.

16

A Different World (1989)

Even while traveling with the family on vacations, my fondness for byways and out-of-the-way places often sets the pace for our trips. In Arizona a few years ago, we saw the Grand Canyon and other familiar attractions. When it was my turn to decide what to see, we headed for the Navajo Nation, formerly called the Navajo Indian Reservation. What we saw was pretty much the rural Southwest with a decidedly Native American flavor. At a routine traffic roadblock, I discovered that the Navajo have their own police force. The roadside stands that feature Indian jewelry took American Express. Poverty seemed to prevail over reasonable standards of living for the most part. It was all very interesting and thought-provoking.

As we crossed the border between Navajo and Hopi territory, we noticed a beautifully carved, wooden sign similar to the signs you see in national and state parks and recreation areas. The text on this sign was very different though. In very serious quasi-legalese, it proclaimed that anyone entering Hopi territory would be subject to the rules and laws of the Hopi tribe. We had no idea what these rules and laws were and proceeded with extreme caution trying to be very discreet. We got through without incident.

The Hopi warning came back to me awhile thereafter as we passed through the gates of Leisure World, a retirement community where my mother-in-law lived. I felt a need to proclaim a "Hopi" warning to the junior members of my own tribe as they visited Leisure World.

It resembles a reservation dedicated to the preservation of life the way it used to be. It is a place where the older generation can still experience life as close to the good old days as possible.

We were there for the Easter Sunday church service. The service was very nice, but I felt as though I had been transported back in time several decades. The elderly couple that greeted us at the door reminded me of some people that used to attend the church I visited as a foreign exchange student years earlier. The layout and content of the program was straight out of the '50s. We were seated in the rear of the sanctuary and, as I surveyed the congregation, I again got that time-warp feeling, seeing all the old ladies with their blue hair only partially concealed by lovely spring hats.

The sermon was gentle and scholarly. The pastor seemed to be striving to fill a ceremonial rather than a spiritual need. If the sermon stirred any emotions, they were no doubt more sentimental than anything else. I do think this may be entirely appropriate so long as these wonderful grandmothers and grandfathers know their final destination, when life on the reservation comes to an end.

The parking lot was again another time warp. Leisure World is located in the middle of Montgomery County outside Washington, D.C., which is yuppie territory. I saw no Mercedeses, BMWs or Japanese imports, just regular domestic big iron, mostly rear-wheel drive. Nothing inside or outside the sanctuary could possibly remind these gentle old folks of these strange new times when women are ordained as ministers and imports from Japan as well as the Old World threaten the domestic industry. At Leisure World, Caprices, Delta 88s, Le Sabres and Impalas still win out over Millenias, Legends, Stanzas and Celicas. Grandma's Volvo 240 DL is an aberration for which I take full responsibility.

Will I ever live in Leisure World? Probably not. I will no doubt hang on to certain traditional values, but I still want to be part of an active, vibrant society. I am more of an observer than an activist, but

I still hope to make a contribution. Progress is not measured only in new things, ideas and trends. Progress is the successful blend of the old and the new. This can be achieved only if the generations are integrated rather than segregated.

17

Life Goes On (1991)

My wife is downstairs watching a TV show called *Life Goes On*. In the meantime, I have been wandering through the house realizing how true that phrase is. Our son is going off to college next week. Our two daughters have gotten engaged this year, and they have announced that they are getting married next spring. We just found out about the last one a few days ago. We are very happy for them, but it will mean major changes – not only for them, but also for us. It will also mean major expenses, I have been told.

I said that I had been wandering through the house, and that really reinforced the life-goes-on feeling. You see, I had been putting up some bookshelves earlier in the day, and I started to look at some of the books that I own. Boy, do they tell a story. The story of my life, I mean. The bookshelves I put up are in one of our closets, and that forced me to look at some of the clothes that I own. It is hard to believe, looking at them today, but I must have worn them at some stage in my life.

Permit me to share some of the phases of my life as I experienced them today, working away in the closet. Don't worry, I did not come across any skeletons and, even if that were the case, I probably would not bother you with them.

One of the books I came across is *New Dress for Success* by John T. Molloy. It was a gift from our corporate training department after my latest promotion. Because I got the promotion first and then the book, I suppose success will be measured by my ability to stay promoted. I have not read the whole book. In fact, I have read only fragments of it. I may be throwing caution to the wind, but my office attire, work clothes if you will, is a combination of what my budget will allow, styles and combinations I consider tasteful, and what I see people in similar jobs wear successfully. I am not suggesting that I ignore Mr. Molloy's advice. I just have not paid all that much attention to it.

I concede, however, that my ties are tied in a half-Windsor knot. They probably were all along. I just had no idea what the knot was called. I tend to prefer rather conservative ties, regimental stripes being one of my favorites, and I do put a dimple in them. It is supposed to signify a man who is careful about his appearance. My wife pays more attention to nostril hairs, but that is a different story entirely.

Molloy's book does say that beige is the most effective raincoat color. He doesn't specify whether that means all kinds of rain, drizzles as well as downpours. My raincoat is gray, and it does repel rain quite nicely. Lee Iacocca has made shirts with contrasting collars acceptable in conservative companies. I am so grateful. Suspenders should always have button fasteners. Mine used to have little clips. I have donated those to charity. I realize the irony in that. Suit pants should always have cuffs, as most of my recent purchases do. These tips come from a section of the book dealing with our image IQ.

If all this leads you to conclude that I am some kind of clothing fanatic, let me set you straight by describing what I found in my closet today. In fact, you should see what I am wearing right now. My closet is full of garments that I used to wear in public. There are two reasons I don't wear them anymore. For one, it is hard to breathe once I get them on and, furthermore, most of them are from an era before natural fibers and earth tones. Bright-colored polyester stuff that no longer fits you does not spell success. So, why do I hang on to it? I tell myself it will come in handy working in the yard or in the garage. It hasn't yet.

Some of the clothes really aren't that bad, except for the fact that they are a couple of sizes too small. They still occupy a place in the closet, because I tell myself that one of these days I am going on a diet, and I will be able to wear them again. Fat chance.

Anyway, I got kind of sentimental today in my closet looking at all these clothes. My body really used to be comfortable in those sizes. And maybe, just maybe, those polyester pants and nylon shirts weren't that bad after all.

The real story of my life, though, came to me looking at all the books. Some are in Swedish. Most of them are in English, with French, German, Latin, Norwegian, Danish and Icelandic thrown in here and there. My academic past is unmistakable. It seems like a very distant past right now.

I am getting ahead of myself. Three writers dominated my childhood reading. Astrid Lindgren with *Pippi Longstocking* is familiar even to American kids. Stories about Pelle, a cat without a tail, never reached these shores, but I enjoyed them when my mother read them to me at bedtime. My most vivid memories are the Indian stories by James Fenimore Cooper that I devoured as a 10-year-old. Little did I know that I would one day live in the land of *The Deerslayer*.

Schoolbooks have their place, of course. Then, between the ages of 21 and 27, everything in my library deals with Swedish and English literature and language. I had my career planned. I was even on my way to becoming an established educator. I suppose it was still useful for this accidental automotive career. It probably gave my communication skills a boost.

I am proud of the books that have my name on them. For a while in the early '70s, I co-authored several textbooks for Swedes to learn English. If I contributed to somebody's education in any lasting way, I'll be very pleased. That was the idea. We did make some money, but not a whole lot.

Then, there was that major move to the States and a new career in the auto industry. The following titles tell the story of my various assignments. *How I Turn Ordinary Complaints Into Thousands of Dollars,*

What To Do With Your Bad Car, Automotive Engineering, Getting Things Done, How To Get Control of Your Time and Your Life, Supervising, In Search of Excellence, The Leadership Challenge. These preceded *Dress for Success*, by the way.

All my reading is not job-related, of course, but I never did live up to the title of Jack Nicklaus' book, *Golf My Way.* My other passions are evidenced by such titles as *Basic Sailing* and *Handbook of Sailing. How Things Work in Your Home and What To Do When They Don't* has saved me many times. When things go wrong, I tell myself *I'm OK, You're OK.* These are the stories of my life, at least some of them. Lately, I have enjoyed the autobiographies of several national leaders.

I hope, though, when it is all said and done, that the book that has guided and shaped me the most is the Bible. I do have several versions of the English Bible, but for me the "original" text is, after all, the Swedish version. The one my dad read aloud.

18
Labels (1993)

I was about to fertilize my lawn the other day. My background and upbringing in Sweden with Lutheran as well as socialistic overtones have made me a person who pays attention to instructions. After all, they are put out by the "authorities." The instructions on the fertilizer bag were formidable. Good grief! Because I was not a chemistry major, I had a hard time figuring out what I was really spreading in my yard. The stern warnings made me nervous, even though I found others rather humorous.

"Harmful if swallowed. Do not get in eyes. Avoid contact with skin." These were warnings I had expected to read, but I wondered about this one: "Do not use on golf courses and sod farms." And, really, why does it say, "Do not apply in Nassau County, New York, between November 1 and May 20"? I did feel safe about the admonition that said, "Do not apply where fish, shrimp, crab and other aquatic life are important resources." Those members of God's creation are not important resources in my back yard, at least not after the long hot summer we were having. Then I read the warning, "It is a violation of federal law to apply this product in a manner which is inconsistent with this labeling." That sounded serious. Could I go to prison, for over-fertilizing my lawn? Would my citizenship application be in jeopardy? I wondered how many otherwise solid, law-abiding citizens had been caught with the wrong fertilizer in the wrong county at the wrong time of the year.

It is really hard to remain law abiding in your garden. We picked up some mums at a local farm market recently. One of them had the following label, "Unauthorized propagation prohibited." It is unlikely that I would be able to violate this rule on my barren soil. I am having a tough time getting weeds to grow.

There are other labels that have given rise to some amusement. You have no doubt heard of the mattress police. "Do not remove this label under penalty of law." Recently, I put on a brand new pair of underpants, Jockey shorts, to be exact. Smack in the middle of the most private section of this rather private garment was a label saying, "Inspected by Carol." I cannot help but wonder sometimes, when I sit next to somebody on an airplane, if his underwear was also inspected by the same anonymous Carol. Fortunately, this label was rather easy to remove. I hope it was not against the law to do so. Other labels are next to impossible to remove. I purchased a pair of sunglasses, which had a price tag affixed to the right lens. It was one of those sticky labels that would only reluctantly yield to paint thinner. This is also the case with the little sticky tags moving companies use to keep track of all your furniture and all the boxes. We have relocated a few times, and we still have a number of things in the garage and the basement with labels intact from two moves back. I have broken my nails trying to remove them.

Some labels are not labels at all, at least not in the literal sense. I am thinking of the how we label and categorize each other: conservative, liberal, hawk, dove, right wing, leftist, and on and on. Some people wear their labels with pride, while others fight to have theirs removed. They perceive the label that people put on them as a slur. When pro-choicers use the word anti-abortionist rather than pro-lifer, there is often a response in kind. That starts the escalation of the war of words, and while the media claim to be impartial, they reveal their bent by the labels they use.

This fall, Native Americans are making a big deal of the various nicknames we use to refer to our professional sports teams. There were demonstrations outside the ballpark when the Braves went to the World Series. New demonstrations have been promised if the Redskins go to the Super Bowl. Depending on who else may go to the Super Bowl, we may have a real crisis on our hands. However, the most likely opponent is some team from the animal kingdom. I can appreciate a certain sensitivity, but unless it is a really awful team, I don't see it as a huge problem. Personally, I have not been offended by the Minnesota Vikings' use of the name of my ancestors. Now, if they were to play as badly as some teams do year after year, it would perhaps be another matter.

Many Native Americans do not seem to mind either. I was reminded of that fact the other day watching the news. There was a big stink made about a toxic waste dump on an Indian reservation. One of the tribesmen was being interviewed by the reporter. As I recall it, he was in favor of the dump, because it would bring needed revenue to the tribe. What caught my eye, though, was the hat he was wearing. He was a football fan. The label on the hat read: "Redskins." The team was having a good season, and he wore the label proudly.

I guess people have hung various labels on me from time to time. Usually I don't mind, but I would like to get rid of the term "hacker." My golf game is improving. There is one label I wear proudly, and that is "Christian." If people want to hang that label on me, it means that I have been obedient.

19

Early Retirement (1998)

I accepted early retirement in 1997.

The company had strengthened the normal package enough to make the financial aspects very compelling. After nearly a quarter century in the hectic and competitive, sometimes brutal, automotive business, I needed a change of pace. The last few years had been at warp speed.

However, I was not prepared for the resulting inner drama. I had given the company my best effort and then some, perhaps at the expense of other things. Performance and results had been my focus.

Suddenly, without deadlines and objectives, I was a rudderless vessel without a destination. In career counseling sessions with subordinates, I had often told them, "It is more important who you are, than what you do." That phrase took on a new and very personal meaning. What was my identity without the title of vice president?

Another factor contributing to my sense of loss was the fact that practically all my friendships had been of a corporate nature. A number of people in the organization had not only been my colleagues but dear friends as well. Would they still be there for me?

Job security had been an issue for me from time to time, particularly in view of repeated reorganizations. The satisfaction of surviving all these corporate restructurings and making it to retirement was quickly replaced by the need to deal with long-term financial security issues. The retirement funds, which I received in a lump sum, now needed to last the rest of our lives.

* * *

A few excerpts from my personal journal will reveal more about my struggle.

8/30/97

This, then, is the start of something new. Left the office last Wednesday. Ken took over. A strange week it has been; thinking about one person's contribution to the whole in a 60,000-person company. A vacation followed by no more operational responsibilities at Volvo. Ever. This is a void I have never had before.

It has been somewhat akin to starting the summer holidays, or perhaps graduating from high school. It means I must do something else for the rest of my life. The Lord will tell me how he wants me to make a difference.

It is hard to let go, though. I checked the retail sales in the system this morning already. It is 7.21 AM.

12/18/97

Two weeks in Rockleigh finished this chapter; the career at Volvo. I did not get to stay at the Clinton Inn, which would have closed the loop nicely. I stayed there on my first trip to Rockleigh in 1975.

Ironies: Had to sign in to enter Building C on my final day. Bought my first map of Bergen County on my final trip there. Bonnie came in for the weekend to attend Helge's party. We went in to the City on Sunday to attend a service at Times Square Church. Closed another loop on Monday visiting Village Volvo; Mike is proud of his Phase III facility.

Said goodbye to Terry and the office on Tuesday.

After I send back the laptop and the credit cards, I'll be done.

Takes getting used to.

1/10/98

Ten days without voice mail and the memo system. What a change of pace. Hard to imagine that I don't have to be concerned about sales and estimates this year. Can't call in sick either, though.

Talked to Walt earlier this week. Steve called also, and Dave and I talk now and then. Denver and Pittsburgh are still in it (NFL playoffs). Good to know the guys are still interested in the old man. Walt used to end our chats with something like, "So long, boss." This time he said, "So long, friend." That made me feel good.

2/19/98

(on cross-country skis)

The Indian Peaks stunned us in their majestic mass beyond the lake. We will definitely be back, both on skis and perhaps with a camper.

Used my old boots and skis. We looked like veterans in our classic gear; Swedish boots and Finnish skis. The trail was not groomed, and it was nice to make our own tracks through fresh powder.

Some thoughts as the wind howled, sending fresh powder in my face:

Twenty years ago I was dealing with the feelings associated with changing careers: "I was supposed to be a teacher, wasn't I? What am I doing here working for Volvo? Should we stay or go back to Sweden?"

Now I am dealing with life-changing decisions as a result of early retirement. "What kind of footprint did I actually leave behind at Volvo? Maybe it is already covered with fresh powder. Did I get the job done, or did I just do things?" . . .

Such was the nature of my thoughts. The timing could have been better, because all this coincided with other major changes in life. Our son moved out and got a place of his own. My mother had to be put in a group home, and we sold our house and moved to a different state. I will spare you all that, at least for now.

In the meantime, it was nice not to have to replace the battery in the travel alarm.

As I am writing this, I am 10 months into retired life. It has been both an adjustment and a restoration period. It is a privilege to be able to plan your life and activities without day-to-day obligations. We have been more physically active, and my health is being restored. I hope to be off the blood-pressure medicine shortly. My weight is reasonable, my stamina is improving and my golf scores are more respectable. But I am not going to be a fairway bum the rest of my life. A reasonable balance is necessary. Nobody is too old to make a contribution. I know the Lord will show me what his plans are for the rest of my life.

20

Home on the Prairie (1998)

We have moved again. This is our eighth move in 35 years of marriage. Some moves have been transoceanic. Others have been a few miles within the same town. It is always a lot of work. It always means a lot of change.

This latest move was on our own terms, meaning it was not inspired by my company. We did not have children or schools to consider. Still, it was not without hassles or headaches. It is not necessary to revisit all the details. We all know that moving companies and real-estate closings require our full measure of patience. Then a northern Virginia termite colony required decisive defensive action the day before the closing. This added to the excitement and raised my blood pressure into the red zone.

We had lived in the Washington, D.C., area for nine years, but we were still wearing nametags at most social gatherings and church functions. Such is life in and around our nation's capital. Because we are not the Florida or Arizona types, we selected Longmont, Colorado, as the place to enter this new phase of our lives. It seems an ideal place for us. The climate is great. The scenery is beautiful. The town with about 60,000 people still retains some of its high-plains, ranch-town character. It is a good antidote to the D.C. Beltway mentality.

Longmont is big enough to have a mall for convenient shopping, yet small enough to get you across town in 10 minutes or less. We may not have Lord and Taylor, or Saks Fifth Avenue, but we can point to a Super 8 Motel on Main Street right next to the Pick'em Up Truck Store. The grain elevators on the outskirts of town represent our high-rise buildings. The town is big enough to rate two exits off the Interstate, yet small enough to have a street called Main Street.

It is big enough to have a symphony orchestra, yet small enough to have cattle grazing within the city limits and feed stores along Main Street.

It is big enough to have the Dow Jones Industrial Average flashing on a lighted sign at an intersection near the main bank building, yet small enough that freight trains stop traffic on several downtown streets.

It is big enough for three municipal golf courses, yet too small to need a beltway.

We do have our own local paper, but we cheer for a football team from another town 30 miles down the Interstate, the Denver Broncos.

We live in a small patio home with a view of a lake with the majestic Rocky Mountains in the background. Across the lake is a small community called Hygiene. It is a town with only two stop signs. Hygiene Cafe is located across the street from Hygiene Feed and Supply and down the street from Shade Tree Repairs. The cafe is the only restaurant in town. It is a two-room establishment. The regular clientele usually occupies the room closest to the entrance. The cook, a nice, middle-aged lady does her work behind a counter in this same room. I love to go there for breakfast. I usually end up in the back room. To get there you pass through a hallway, where the restroom is found. The restroom includes a bathtub. The walls of the cafe are decorated with photos and paintings of the cafe. Cowboy hats and cowboy boots are normal attire. If people wear baseball caps, they are less often decorated with sports team logos. Rather, they show the names of feed stores and fertilizers. The cinnamon buns are the size of compact discs with mountain topography. The pancakes are often too large to fit on the plate, and the bacon is cooked to perfection. The waitresses know the customers by name. I hope I am regarded as one of the regulars.

We love our new home and new environment, and God's people have welcomed us into fellowship in a local church.

21

The Reunion (1999)

It was with hesitation but, after some gentle nudging from me, my wife signed up for us to attend her 40th high school reunion. I am so glad we went. The event itself was very nice, and the perspective it offered on life is reassuring and unnerving at the same time. We left Colorado on a beautiful summer day and headed east toward Washington, D.C., with a weather forecast that promised heat and high humidity that would drive the heat index to about 105 degrees.

We knew we had found the right hotel, the Gaithersburg Marriott in Maryland, when I saw two fellows unload their cars from two covered trailers. The cars, a street rod and a dragster, looked as if they had come directly from the high school parking lot in 1959. They would certainly provide the appropriate atmosphere and also allow two 57-year-old boys to show off their toys. As I approached the entrance, a showroom-condition '55 Bel Air convertible rounded out the automotive props.

Dancing does not come easily to me because I totally lack rhythm, but I had promised my wife that I would do my best to accommodate her desire to dance. Despite my totally inept attempts at being suave, she seemed to enjoy it. To my surprise, so did I. In between, I tried to slip into a role of inconspicuous observer.

You have to love a reunion where the 57-year-old cheerleader is still called Kissie. Furthermore, she still looked the part. Although most people at the reunion were born within 12 months of each other, there appeared to be at least a 15-year age difference. The ladies seemed to carry their age better than the fellows, or perhaps I am just getting old. The guy who had been married three times danced his heart out and seemed to be contemplating a fourth time by the end of the evening.

Attire ranged from blue jeans to business suits and fancy dresses. Some people struggled to accommodate nature, as George Washington put it in his rules of etiquette. I wondered what some of the ladies would have given to be 50 pounds lighter for this occasion when some of them would see, for the first time in 40 years, the old classmates who had made them swoon back in the '50s. Yet, when the old familiar tunes beckoned them to dance, gravity did not seem to matter. They rocked around the oldies on light stocking feet. The disc jockey knew exactly what would stir the emotions and bring back memories. Elvis and Buddy Holley came over the speakers from today's CD albums rather than the old 45s. As I sat back and took it all in, these middle-age grandmas were somehow transformed into 18-year-olds in poodle skirts and bobby socks. The guys needed to suck in their stomachs, but their balding heads could almost have passed for crew cuts.

Even some teachers made it to the reunion. The assistant football coach still looked capable of sacking any quarterback. The blue-haired chorus teacher was adorable in leading us in the Alma Mater. She did so with gusto, but only after telling everybody to be quiet so she could give us the right pitch.

The line at the roast beef table was twice as long as the one at the pasta bar. I felt I was among peers. We all indulged in ice cream with toppings, basic vanilla and chocolate. Forget the calories and the cholesterol for this one night. We were young and life was only beginning.

22

A Clean Land (2000)

With tears welling in his eyes, the Native American looked at a once serene piece of nature. Now it was littered with bottles and cans. Pieces of paper were blowing in the wind. The camera lingered on the man's face, and you could see tears running down his cheeks. This was the setting of an ad in an environmental campaign several years ago.

Many Americans were compelled to action regarding trash and litter. Organizations all across this land have adopted sections of highways, which they keep tidy and free of litter. Other activities have resulted in an essentially cleaner America. In most cases, this is because people care. In other cases, it is because of stiff fines. In Texas, for example, the fine for littering is $1,000, and the signs read, "Don't Mess With Texas."

I envision another vignette today of one of our Founding Fathers experiencing feelings of sadness and disgust similar to those of the Native American's, as the Founding Father looks at the moral decay, the littering of our minds, in modern society.

A lot has changed since my initial experiences as an exchange student in the '50s to my current situation as a retired naturalized citizen early in the 21st century. Even without looking at the '50s through rose-colored lenses, it is easy to see that morals and behavior have changed. Indeed, sometimes it appears that the old moral code has been erased.

The Founding Fathers based this nation on Judeo-Christian values and ethics. Even if the president still takes the oath of office with his hand on the Bible, public discourse and public behavior are often in sharp contrast to the old ideals. Sadly, this is sometimes true for the president himself. You see the evidences of change everywhere – in classrooms, in boardrooms, in our legislative chambers, in our courtrooms and in the media.

We need to get back on course. This nation is in treacherous moral waters, but it can survive, if we once again steer by the compass our Founding Fathers used, and which was given to us by our Creator.

My faith in America and Americans gives me confidence that we can do it. It will take individual moral strength and courage to challenge what is currently politically correct. The political system will not correct the problems, but I hope it will not stand in the way when individuals and families all across this land stand up for what they believe and for what is right. The many individual acts of kindness, courage and moral strength that I have discovered and experienced in America, my adopted country, give me hope. It is my hope I can live up to my pledge of allegiance by acting in a similar way.

23

The Things We Say (2000)

"Don't kill the ball. Just make contact."

"Good eye. Good eye."

Those words are echoing countless times every summer from around thousands of Little League ball fields all across this land. As with most clichés, they help define the character of the land and its people.

They also help define the game, which I find, paradoxically, to be so genuinely American, and somewhat non-American at the same time. To love baseball, even without a full understanding of the many nuances of the game, is almost a patriotic duty. Yet the pastoral scenes that the games provide are in sharp contrast to the hustle and bustle that goes on in our modern society. It has been pointed out by George Carlin and others that hockey and football are perhaps a better representation of life in our cities, in the business world and in politics. Even the baseball uniforms are oddly anachronistic, harkening back to another era. The idiom of the game, however, has enriched our language.

"Play ball," we say, and the phrase has transcended the game itself, as have many other sports idioms. You don't need to play baseball to hit a "home run" anymore, or to be "way out in left field," for that matter.

I think it is also fair to say that our language is richer with such idioms as "circle the wagons," which reconnects us with a rich heritage. It reminds us of the efforts and struggles as well as sacrifices of those who have gone before us. It wasn't always "easy sailing." "No pain, no gain," so "grin and bear it." Rugged individualism, "be your own man," as well as extraordinary collective efforts made and shaped this country. Values were passed down through generations. Indeed, "like father, like son" should always be a positive reflection of a solid upbringing. I am afraid the phrase is not always used that way.

What sort of idioms, then, will endure from these postmodern times? Are there any words or phrases, besides "Watergate" and its many derivatives that will live on, phrases that we can be proud of passing on?

At the dawn of a new century, when traditional values are threatened and truth is challenged in the public square, one may begin to wonder. Let us not lose hope, though. Even when public figures and national leaders behave with reckless disregard for the truth, there are, of this I am convinced, enough individuals throughout this land who have not abandoned the truth. Those are the people who say, "Oh, my God" or "God help me," not just as idioms but also with personal conviction. This must be our legacy, and He will not let us down.

PART FOUR

Trying to Obey the Lord

24

Another Season of Life

Old age is the most unexpected of
all the things that happen to a man.
                                    Leon Trotsky

A variety of options came to mind after I accepted early retirement at the end of 1997. Do I get another job or spend a lot of time sailing? Maybe I should get serious about playing golf. The last two options appealed to me. After all, the job had started to wear on me and some health issues had arisen; increased blood pressure was one of them. Being part of the executive group as well as running one of Volvo's regional offices had been fun and exciting, but it had taken its toll.

Bonnie had been involved in a short-term ministry trip to Russia and wanted me to join her in looking into other similar opportunities. My initial response was, "I can't deal with that now. I need at least two years to recover."

Other thoughts also went through my head such as, "Russia! Really?" As I pondered her suggestion, some childhood experiences came to mind. During my preschool years, Grandma Gerda had two favorite phrases when she thought I needed to calm down a bit. "You are as wild as a Russian" was something I heard often. When I was really out of control, she would say, "You better behave, or the Russians will come and take you away."

When I was a bit older, we had the news reports about Russian submarines prowling the waters along the east coast of Sweden. One of them ran aground once somewhere in the southern part of the Baltic Sea. By the way, it was one their "Whiskey" class subs and the joke was, "Whiskey on the rocks."

Then during my infantry days, the premise for the war games was always "the Kingdom has been attacked from the east." That, of course, meant the Soviets.

So I had my reservations, but the Lord eventually made me realize what he had already revealed to Bonnie. Because I had taught English in the Swedish school system and did not want to return to corporate life, I looked into working at some language camps in Russia, teaching English. Then I ran into one major obstacle. The groups in the States that ran these camps found me unqualified, because English was not my native language. That was a little hard to accept for a certified English teacher.

Eventually, we connected with the International School Project and were able to work with teachers in Russia and later Ukraine. Over the years, we attended many conferences dealing with morals and ethics, and character education. I also had the privilege to direct a few of them.

As we prepared for the first trip to central Russia, the conference was suddenly cancelled. Instead, we were welcome to attend another conference in Siberia. I had some reservations about Siberia, this being our first experience with ISP, but after all it was summer, so we went ahead. It proved to be a wonderful experience, and of course the teachers were not at all like the Russians my grandma had threatened me with. We now have many friends all over Russia and Ukraine, and with the ISP curriculum we shared with them, they are able to guide their students with principles based on the Christian worldview.

It was a privilege for both of us to take part in these conferences for a number of years. We are not in a position to travel there these days, but we stay in touch with many of the teachers in those countries and cherish their friendship.

25

The Five Love Languages

It was a special privilege to travel as a couple. With a few exceptions, this had not been the case during my time with Volvo. What we didn't realize at first was the fact that the teachers, most of whom were women, paid close attention to how Bonnie and I interacted. Evidently, we made enough of an impression on a few of them that we were told we ought to write a book on love and marriage.

That did not materialize, but it led to the two of us giving a lecture at several of the conferences titled "Success in Marriage and Showing Love." As we shared the story of our transatlantic romance and the fact that we came from such different backgrounds, we wove it into the theme of the book *The Five Love Languages* by Gary Chapman. This book was handed out to the teachers at most of the conferences. I am sure Mr. Chapman's book was extremely helpful to the teachers. We hope, of course, that what we shared of a personal nature helped as well.

Bonne and I alternated the various comments, and we started out by describing our life and family. We then went on with Bonnie having a female interpreter while mine was male. Here is how it went.

Leif: *We have also discovered something else about love. Love is not primarily just a feeling.*

Bonnie: *Neither is it a matter of whether you are in love or out of love with someone. Some research shows that the in-love experience for most couples* *lasts on the average about two years. The highest kind of love is a decision to want and to act for the well-being of another. Let me repeat that.*

The focus is not on what I want or need but on desiring and doing what is best for the other. So if this is the definition of real love, let's think a moment about how we do this love. One of our most basic needs as human beings is to experience love and acceptance, to know we matter to someone else, that we are basically OK as a person. Love and acceptance, or the opposite, rejection, are communicated by how we are treated and what is said to us or done for us or to us.

Leif: *There are five main love languages that say these things, and we all need to EXPERIENCE LOVE in all five ways. But there seems to be one language that communicates most clearly to us. It is our main love language. We need to hear it communicated frequently to feel emotionally that we are loved and appreciated. Language is about communication.*

Usually our actions and attitudes communicate more than what we actually say. The book you received deals with how we communicate love. It has applications with other members of the family. And it is not limited to family – it applies to showing love and care to your students also. So let's look at these five love languages, and we will try to give you some examples from our 43 years together.

Bonnie: *Spending* **quality time** *together is one of these five love languages. People are so busy and separate these days that we must schedule time to be together. Just sitting beside each other and looking at television is not enough, but we do some of that, too. It does not provide the focused attention that really tells our spouse that we care about them.*

So we try to schedule one day every week to do something we enjoy together. Because we live very close to the Rocky Mountains, we like to go up there to hike in the summer or cross-country ski in the winter.

Leif: *The other days of the week we often do other things together. We might walk around the lake near our house. Sometimes it is just a project around the house, or doing errands together.*

Bonnie: *A large part of focused attention is learning the art of effective communication. This is a dialect of quality time together. Because we are different, there are many times we must talk things through. Focused attention* *in quality conversation as we spend time together requires learning good listening skills. When Leif is angry with me or irritated, I must acknowledge his right to be angry and allow him to tell me about it. I can more easily hear him if he uses – "I feel" or "I need" statements rather than – "you always" or "you never" that accuse me of something. I can get defensive. I must practice not interrupting him. I have so many more words as a woman that I tend to do that too often. If Leif feeds back to me what he thinks I have said, I can correct him so I am not misunderstood, so I don't hurt him. If I really feel I have been heard, then I feel loved.*

Leif: *I am not very good at this.*

Bonnie: *But with practice, I think we are both getting better at it all the time.*

Leif: *Controlling my own anger is a vital part of any relationship. Both explosive and implosive anger are harmful. Yelling, accusing, criticizing, throwing things are destructive of relationships.*

Bonnie: *Anger turned inward may look like the silent treatment but may lead to depression or ulcers.* **Giving gifts** *can be an expression of love.*

Leif: *This means that the gift cannot be a reward for desired behavior or a change bargained for; that's manipulation. These gifts are best given with special care in presentation, at an appropriate time, perhaps even in the presence of others. Bonnie makes me Swedish dried buns (skorpor) for each special remembrance day, like birthday or anniversary.*

Bonnie: *Leif likes to get me earrings for my special days, because he knows they will please me.*

Leif: *Here is a trick we have learned from another couple on giving an expensive flower bouquet. If we are in the store together, I may pick out a very nice bouquet and very ceremoniously hand it to Bonnie. Then when we are done shopping, we put it back before we leave. We have created an occasion that speaks love, and it hasn't cost anything. People who see us may think we are crazy, but that is OK.*

Bonnie: Touch *is another of the five love languages. It is extremely important for maintaining a healthy environment in marriage. We are not referring to sexual touching; that is not within the scope of this talk. But affectionate touching communicates emotional love. Leif may hug me or rub my shoulders.*

Leif: *Bonnie often holds my hand when we walk together. But touch as a love language is not limited to husband and wife. It is a great way we shared our love with our children when they were small. It is needed by teens, too, but not in the presence of their peers. Teens will often communicate with body gestures when they will welcome or reject touching; it can include hugging, wrestling, a pat on the back or a touch on the shoulder.*

Bonnie: *For a teen child, it seems to be more accepted in private, when home from a difficult day, or in different ways than when they were children. Timing is everything as well as finding new appropriate ways to touch that respect their individuality and emerging adulthood.*

Leif: *Dads must hug their daughters and sons, but they will often be moody and hard to understand. This is because they struggle with teen issues of self-identity and the need to gain independence from parents.*

Bonnie: Words of encouragement *that replace critical ones are essential for filling the emotional love tank of anyone. Being appreciated for success, or honest effort, is more important than perfection in anything we try to do.*

Leif: *Lately I have tried my hand at writing. With some success, the newspaper in our town has hired me to write articles for it. Not news articles but opinion pieces, and she is always interested in hearing about what I am writing. And she comes up with very useful suggestions sometimes. She tells me it is very good, or right on.*

Bonnie: *He tries to support me with words of encouragement when I minister to the elderly and those in jail.*

Leif: *You are good at one on one.*

Bonnie: *And he often compliments me on the meals I prepare for us. Those words of appreciation fill my emotional love tank. We all want our spouse to respect us. We owe respect to all persons just because everyone is made in God's image. We owe it to each other. Harsh, abusive, critical words attack a person instead of building up. They are very destructive in relationships.*

Leif: *Trust, however, is something that must be earned by the other even though it is good to communicate that I desire to be trustworthy and that I want to trust. We must be honest with each other when we have done* *something wrong. We have to admit it and ask for forgiveness. The willingness and ability to forgive come from God.*

Bonnie: *The return of trust can be earned by demonstrating a change in the behavior that broke the trust, at least on my part. It makes it easier for the other person to grant forgiveness and to be reconciled.*

Leif: *The fifth language of love is* **acts of service.** *It is essential in showing love to a spouse that we serve each other by helping with tasks that need to get done.*

Bonnie: *A small example: My eyesight is very poor so he helps me thread the needle.*

Leif: *So that she can sow on the buttons I lose.*

Bonnie: *He also carries in the groceries, and puts out the garbage.*

Leif: *She makes me the food I like.*

Bonnie: *He takes care of things and fixes what breaks.*

Leif: *She washes and irons my clothes. She cuts my hair.*

Bonnie: *You know Leif, there isn't that much left to cut.*

Leif: *DreamMakers/DreamBreakers curriculum] deals with the subject of success in marriage. We recommend it as a complement to the lesson yesterday. One of the key concepts in the lesson deals with how a young person treats a parent or sibling of the opposite sex. This is a good predictor of how he or she will treat his or her spouse. The lesson also focuses on the qualities that a young person can develop to achieve success in marriage.*

Qualities they can work on now to help them prepare for the future, as was the case in Lesson 16. Another important part of Lesson 20 is to help teens guard the door of their heart. That is, to save themselves sexually for their future spouse. God's way of one man, one woman for life is the best way to avoid heartbreak. But we must encourage young people to act wisely and choose carefully. A well-known American psychologist, Dr. James Dobson, has said: "Marry the one you know you cannot live without. Don't just look for the one you think you may be able to live with." *Here is another piece of advice from another source:* "Keep your eyes wide open before marriage but half-closed after marriage."

PART FIVE

Exercising Personal Options

26

Time to Relax

He makes me lie down in green pastures.
Psalm 23

If there is such a thing as having too many hobbies, I may be someone people could point to in order to make that case. Then again, as a retired person, I have more time to spend on hobbies. Most of the leisure activities these days are done with my wife. I think that should count as a mitigating circumstance.

Golf is not one of the things we do together, which means I need to exercise some discipline as to how much time I spend on the driving range or the golf course. That is probably just as well, because my future in golf is not what I once dreamed it would be. No, I am not thinking of the PGA; far from it. My handicap is really creeping in the opposite direction of where it was once headed. I still enjoy the game, and still refer to it as golf. Some would probably use another term.

We did have to give up sailing once we moved away from the Chesapeake Bay area. Yes, there are lots of lakes in Colorado, but once you are used to heading from Annapolis to St. Michaels or Oxford on Maryland's Eastern Shore, it is hard to settle for the other side of some local reservoir. Only the archipelago near my Swedish hometown could measure up.

We have put a lot of miles on cars and RVs since retirement. For us, it is often the journey that counts more than the destination. Avoiding the Interstate highways and exploring the country via back roads is a great way to travel. There is a lot to be gained by spending time in what is often flyover country. And, yes, people do survive without fast-food outlets on every street corner. Some of the "on the road" stories in this part did, indeed, take place before retirement. I would call them practice runs before we could dedicate more time to one of our favorite activities.

We still do some cross-country skiing. These days, it is more like dragging our feet in snow. It has been almost 30 years since our last Governor's Cup 10K race. Even then, we weren't really competing; we just tried to finish the race.

Hiking on the wonderful mountain trails nearby is not as easy as it once was, but we still manage now and then, at times even with snowshoes. They were a gift from the kids when we turned 70, probably a subtle message that it was time to slow down.

Another reason for slowing down was the onset of Parkinson's disease in my late 60s. The symptoms are still fairly manageable and, to a degree, controlled with medicine, and I have learned that staying active will slow down the progression of the disease. When the doctor told me to remember to swing my arms to avoid stiffness, I decided that was as good a reason as any to keep playing golf even though the scores are not what they used to be. The doctor agreed and told me to play twice a week. It sure beats going to physical therapy, although I do that with some regularity as well.

There are a bunch of things I can no longer do, but I have learned to look at the bright side. There are also things I no longer have to do. I have the support of the extended family and many chores around the house can be turned over to the grandkids.

In this context, Psalm 23 has taken on a new dimension. I am trying to look at this disease as a "green pasture," knowing the Lord "restores my soul" and gives me rest and a new perspective "beside quiet waters."

27

Cash or Credit (1992)

It was a late afternoon in August. My wife and I had been sailing for a couple of hours. We were heading southwest toward Annapolis on a port tack. There was a steady wind from the south, waves were less than one foot, the humidity was moderate, and because it was a weekday, we were almost alone on Chesapeake Bay. I spotted a couple of other sailboats coming out from the Severn River. The only powerboat in sight was a huge freighter at anchor farther south, near the Thomas Point light. In the distant haze, I could make out the dome of the state capitol.

We had a full main and genoa and, when the wind picked up a little, our 25-footer heeled to almost 45 degrees and picked up speed. I heard the bow surging through the water, the glorious sound of pollution-free speed. I listened to the merry clucking sound of the displaced water coming together again in the wake. It was a perfect day for a sailing enthusiast. It was made even more perfect when my wife announced that we were going to have fresh corn on the cob with our barbecued chicken that evening.

My wife dozed off for a while, and I was alone with my thoughts. These were not profound thoughts of global and eternal consequence, I admit. The main thing that occupied my mind was this: "There is something basically honest about a wooden tiller." Sure, there is pedestal steering with rack and pinion. But with my nicely sculpted piece of wood bolted directly to the rudder, I had total control of this vessel. I sheeted in the main, leaned back a little, took in the gentle breeze and waited for the next puff, enjoying the entire experience. There are fancier boats than mine, and they are starting to use terms like push-button sailing, but I enjoy the basic pleasures of wind propulsion. For me, tiller-steering is a must.

There are many other similar distinctions between basic equipment and fancy, complex modern solutions. My 1959 Volvo has a manual choke, for example. I pull it out and a cable influences the carburetor, directly and without any complications. Modern cold-start systems are dependent on temperature sensors for coolant and ambient temperature, air-mass meters, speed sensors, an idle speed-control valve, and often a cold-start injector and an oxygen sensor. All this is part of a fuel-management system, which in turn is controlled by a microprocessor. If something goes wrong, a federally mandated "check engine" light comes on, and you need fault-tracing equipment costing several thousand dollars. Modern cars don't get fixed in your drive way under a shade tree with basic hand tools. I mourn the demise of the manual choke. It was such an honest device, and the federal government trusted me to operate it.

These days when you go to the parts department of an automotive dealership, the clerk is likely to look up the part you need using an electronic parts catalog. What was wrong with that impressive array of books that used to run the length of the counter? I was always impressed how quickly they were able to look up the part I needed, flipping the pages with such dexterity to arrive at the proper page in a matter of seconds. Such actions inspire confidence and trust.

When I take the car in for service, my personal data as well as make, model, color, vehicle identification number and mileage are punched into a computer along with whatever service or repair is needed. The printer goes *brrzzt*, and the repair order falls conveniently on the counter for my authorization signature. When I pick up the car, the cashier runs my credit card through a slot in a device that is hooked up to the bank. The computer at the bank knows me intimately and, after a few seconds, it usually approves my spending.

It is all very convenient, effortless, impersonal and at a very high interest rate, unless you pay off the entire balance within 30 days. I have become so used to automatic teller machines, computerized billing procedures and bar codes at the checkout counter that I have almost forgotten how it used to be.

The other day my son took me to the computer lab at his university. He showed me all the equipment – about 50 different machines – and what you can do with them. I was amazed by his knowledge and his enthusiasm, as well as by these machines and their capability. He was even able to check the availability of certain books in the library of a different university. I felt ignorant and like a real old-timer in this new world of technical wonders. As we left the room, however, I saw something that made me feel a little better. There on the wall, just by the door, was an old-fashioned, hand crank pencil sharpener – a relic from my own school days, but a symbol to me that some things don't change, and some things don't really need improving.

My faith in old-fashioned values, trust, simplicity and honesty got another boost the other day. It started with a flat tire on my daughter's car, the left rear, tubeless Michelin radial tire. We jacked up the car, removed the wheel and took it over to the local Amoco station. Fortunately it is still a service station, which means they work on cars, rather than sell potato chips and soft drinks. I discovered a nail in the tire and, although it had 45,000 miles on it, I felt it was worth repairing. You are supposed to get more than 50,000 miles out of a Michelin. The guy at the gas station promised to take a look at it that same evening. There were no computer entries, not even a repair order. They did not ask my name. When I returned the following day, the man I had talked to the night before was not there. The new fellow had me point out which tire was mine from among a bunch of tires sitting there in the shop area of the gas station. I picked out a really good one. Just kidding, it *was* my tire. The man carried it out to the car and put it in the trunk. He told me the repair was $7. They had put a rubber plug in it. I handed him a

$10 bill. He took out a wad of bills from his pocket, peeled off three dollars, handed them to me and told me to have a nice day. The entire transaction was satisfying. Not only did I not have to buy a new tire, but also the situation was filled with trust, honesty, human warmth and a minimum of hassle. I am not sure how long this piece of idyllic nostalgia will last. The owner told my wife recently that they are going to computerize the pumps, and he was not entirely happy about it. He was losing contact with his customers. They will pay at the pump by just swiping their cards. This is kind of distressing to us old-timers. Have no fear, though. The other day I found out how even these modern gas stations check to see how much gas they have in their underground tanks. There is no digital readout. They use a long wood stick that they lower through a hole into the tank, and they check to see how much of the stick gets wet. I think that is wonderful.

28

Back to School (1992)

My son is a sophomore at Radford University in southern Virginia. I took him back to school after the summer this past weekend. It took some doing. He has a four-door 1977 Volvo sedan with a decent size trunk. It was not nearly enough. I had to borrow a full-size, extended-cab Ford pickup truck.

Besides clothes, books, and sports equipment, he took the following items along:

one bookcase
one desk with hutch
one chair
two lamps
two electric fans
one "loft bed"
one refrigerator
one computer
one monitor
one printer
one telephone
one answering machine
one multiple piece stereo system
one Super Nintendo Game

As we headed south, both vehicles were jammed full, and two pieces of the loft bed extended behind the 8-foot-long bed of the truck. As I came around the entrance ramp to Interstate 66, the load shifted a little. I turned my head to check and realized how my son's college experience has given a whole new meaning to school supplies. Gone are the days when, at the beginning of each school year, I would accompany him to the drug store. Whatever it was he needed, such as pencils, pens, protractor, notebooks, etc., we usually managed to fit all of it into one plastic bag. Nowadays we need a small motorcade, and he is still in a shared dorm room. What's going to happen if he rents an apartment off campus?

College life is not simple, but I mused over the added complexity my son was bringing to the situation. We had not brought an electrician along, and I was hoping he could master the wiring of all this equipment. If not, there are circuit breakers for safe measure.

I did not mind the 500-mile round trip. I rather enjoy life on the highway. In this slightly aging truck, I had a commanding view of my surroundings and felt almost like a genuine Bubba. I dialed in WMZQ 98.7 FM, "Washington's hot new sound in country music." I thought it would add the appropriate flavor and drown out any thought of corporate objectives and deadlines. The fact that the air-conditioner did not work and the truck lacked cruise control provided additional realism. You are not supposed to be that comfortable in a truck, and a little bit of suffering would probably do me good. I had not shaved that morning. A smooth face would have looked out of place. My doctor has told me to keep my face out of the sun, so I wear a straw hat occasionally. On this particular day, it made my costume complete. There was no gun rack in the truck.

The trip went well. I had to return home before the room was completely assembled. Later, I received assurance that everything was OK and in working order. I do know that the answering machine was functioning. Incidentally, I discovered that we were not the only ones to test the capacity of the dorm rooms. One of the coeds had brought an exercise machine that simulates stair-climbing. I found it ironic as she struggled to fit this device into the dorm elevator.

My taste for country music was rekindled in the truck. I cannot say that I am really passionate, but I enjoy it. I like country stations also because they are so powerful. You don't have to change the dial constantly as you drive down the highway. The heart and soul of the land is coming through loud and clear with unabashed wattage as you cover mile after mile.

This was comforting to me during a cross-country trip a week later. The land and its people are still true to their roots. Gospel stations are a close second for coast-to-coast coverage, while the typical urban new-age stations often fade away as you travel through the heartland. This is also reassuring. On my trip I got off the Interstates at least twice a day. The Interstates are a superimposed grid choking the land. As they speed transportation, they divide farms and villages, slicing through creation without regard for local patterns and traditions. Taking the time to change the tempo of the trip on smaller roads is vital to my well-being. I reconnect with the land and its people. I sense the soul of America with the air-conditioning off and the windows open. The smell of manure and skunks along with freshly cut grain is medicine for me.

I took a picture of the post office in Crawley, West Virginia. It was housed in a modest trailer. The U.S. flag was flying from the pole next to the parking lot. The trailer is serving the citizens of Crawley the same way a huge marble building in Washington, D.C., does. It receives the same federal backing and the price of the stamp is the same no matter the overhead.

In New Baden, Illinois, I stopped for food at Rita's and Jerry's Restaurant. I ate too much, of course. How can you pass up a full-course dinner, including coffee and dessert, for less than five dollars? If Rita and Jerry are not worried about cholesterol, why should I be? Besides, their regular customers seemed so wholesome and looked so healthy.

It took me awhile to find a pay phone in Russell, Kansas. Eventually, I located one next to the grain elevator of the co-op. It may have been the only pay phone in town. The locals seemed amused when I asked for directions to a phone. "Why is this fellow in such a hurry to talk to somebody?" After a few days on the road, I began to wonder the same thing. The office seemed to be getting along well enough without me. I started out again enjoying the cornfields and the sunflowers even more.

As you travel the byways of America, you sense that most small towns are characterized by essentially three public buildings – the courthouse, a church or churches, and the post office. Often you have to ask directions to the post office, which is frequently tucked away on a side street. You can often find the churches easily enough, because of their size and architecture. However, it is the courthouse that occupies the dominant, often central, site in town. This is sad. Is it God's grace or man's law that influences our society most?

29

Corn (1995)

My wife loves corn on the cob. She grew up in Maryland where plenty of fresh corn every summer shaped her taste. While we lived in Colorado in the '80s, she suffered severe withdrawal symptoms. We tried to grow corn in the back yard with little success. We did not have the right soil, and the climate was too dry. Living in Sweden during the early part of our marriage was even worse, from a corn point of view. There, even the canned corn was inferior to the canned corn she was used to.

We now live in northern Virginia, and my wife is again able to satisfy her habit. Every summer, during July and August, she goes into this "a person needs corn on the cob to survive" kind of mood. She sniffs out fresh corn within a 40-mile radius of the nation's capital. She tends to favor, or more accurately, it has to be corn grown on the Eastern Shore of Maryland. During the high season, she will settle for nothing less than Silver Queen corn. Fortunately, the Maryland highways are dotted with produce stands where enterprising farmers sell fresh corn as well as fruit and vegetables. Our favorite one is along Highway 214, which is Central Avenue extended between Washington, D.C., and Annapolis. On the way to our sailboat in Annapolis, we often go out of our way to visit this particular stand.

Today, my wife was dozing as I pulled up to the stand. It did not take her long to wake up. She bounced out of the car. I watched as she approached the stand. She had a confident, determined gait on light, happy feet. She surveyed the corn with her eyes and fingers, testing several kernels with her nails. The farmer did not seem to mind. He knew he was dealing with an expert, and he also knew that his corn would stand up to the scrutiny of the most discerning customer. "Was this corn picked today?" Her usual question got a positive answer. The smile on her face was unmistakable as she walked back to the car with a dozen ears in a plastic bag. Neither was there any doubt what we were having for dinner. She often cooks two ears for each person, as was the case today after a day of sun and sailing on the Chesapeake. I normally eat one. Somehow there is seldom any left. I wonder where it all goes.

As far as craving goes, this is a pretty harmless one. Fresh corn on the cob, dripping with butter, and seasoned with salt and pepper, eaten hot out of the pot does not harm people around you. Neither does it fry your brain cells, and it is legal. I don't know how healthy it is for the body, with clogged arteries and all that stuff, you know. I do know that it is honest food, which is good for the soul.

30

Perfect Strangers (1996)

We were on one of our cross-country trips between Colorado and Virginia. This was before our move to Longmont after the fast-paced life in the Capital area. We wanted to savor the trip, so we abandoned Interstate 70 for lesser-known back roads of Kansas, perched high above passenger-car level in the cab of our 1994 Ford F-150. Highway 9 runs parallel to U.S. 36 in northern Kansas and was marked as a scenic route. We got on Highway 9 near Dresden. It turned out to be an excellent choice. We maintained a reasonable speed, and there was not a lot of traffic to contend with.

After glimpsing several small Kansas towns, such as Lenora, Densmore, Logan and Speed, we spotted Kirwin Reservoir on our right. We debated whether to pull off and enjoy a picnic next to the lake or try our luck in a local restaurant. We decided to go for the local flavor. A few miles farther down the road, we found Gaylord, a small town without paved streets and with a limited choice of restaurants. The hitching posts were gone, but we parked our vehicle the way they used to tie their horses – that is, diagonally – with the front toward an elevated sidewalk. Gaylord is quite obviously not a tourist town, and we were likely the only folks from out of town. The words chic or charming would not enter your mind trying to describe it. That suited me fine. Furthermore, Paradise was just 35 miles south along Highway 18.

About half past one, we walked into the only eating establishment we could find. It turned out to be my kind of place. There were about 10 tables, and from any one of them, you could glimpse the kitchen. You couldn't talk about decor, but there were some pictures on the walls, a couple of calendars, and posters about upcoming auctions and farm shows. The dishes and the utensils were not fancy, just basic and solid. Everything pointed to the fact that the place attracted and maintained its customer base by the food itself, rather than the presentation or, for that matter, the ambience of the dining room.

As we looked over the menu, the prices made us feel as if we were in a foreign country with a very favorable exchange rate. We decided to make it our main meal for the day. Furthermore, the menu did not have the little heart signs to remind you that you are supposed to count calories and worry about cholesterol.

We were in the middle of our meal and enjoying the whole experience when the owner came over to our table. At that point, we were the only customers in the place, and we realized that the staff had left as well.

"Would you folks mind locking up when you leave, since I have to go to a meeting?"

"We'll be glad to. When do you normally close?"

"Oh, we usually close around two o'clock."

"Really, why is that?"

"Well, we serve breakfast in the morning, of course. Then the ranch hands come here for lunch. That is our normal day."

"We'll close when we leave. Thank you so much. The food is wonderful."

We were warmed by the trust shown two complete strangers. It was such a contrast to what we were used to in the big city. As I finished my meal, I thought it tasted even better than before.

Small town America had made a lasting impression on my soul. My eyes took in the place one more time, as I pushed the door shut.

Maybe we should have done the dishes, too.

In summer 1958, I listened to President Eisenhower address several hundred of us exchange students on the South Lawn of the White House. He occupies a special place in my memory since he took time to speak to us.

In winter 1957, I went on a skiing vacation to the hills of Maryland with my host family, Dr. J. Thomas and Mrs. Vivian Schnebley. Bonnie, center, was observing me closely, as were sister Sharon and brother John.

Left: Aboard a ship steaming down the St. Lawrence River toward Europe, I take a moment to reflect on the year just behind me as a foreign exchange student in the United States. At the same time, I am looking into my future and asking myself whether I would ever see my host family again. I had grown up considerably and was a changed young man. My future also was changing, and the answer to my question was: I would return.

After being apart for a year, who was happier, me or my parents, Arne and Majken, at the dock in Holland?

Above: I was able to see in person Detroit's "big iron" with their "dollar-grin" grilles in the late 1950s. Below: The more modest Volvos arrived in America, and later models populated my growing family in the 1990s.

Left: I turned 18 years old in America and celebrated with my exchange brothers, John, center, and Bob, who eagerly watches to see whether I can blow out all the candles in one breath. I think I did.

Right: My exchange brother, Bob, and I were the same age, and he became the brother I never had. So working together on projects like painting the family garage came naturally. Two years later, in the summer of 1959, he came to visit me in Sweden, and we toured Europe, in a Volvo, of course.

Above: Home from the swearing-in ceremony and an American citizen at last, I am proud to be an American and wear the Stars and Stripes. Below: Bonnie and I celebrate my new citizenship and new allegiance.

Above: Bonnie celebrates with four of our grandchildren before they became teen-agers. Below: A few years later, a second granddaughter came along. Bonnie spends time with Mia in our home in Longmont, Colorado.

These photos show only two of my many pastimes. Above: I am sailing on Chesapeake Bay with Thomas Point Lighthouse in the distant background. At left: I am relaxing at home with our children, from left to right, Melinda, Thomas and Katrina, when they were teenagers.

Above: At an International School Project seminar in Vinnitsya, Ukraine, in 2006, Bonnie and I present a talk on the Five Love Languages and how they apply to our marriage. Left: Bonnie and I were honored at the end of an ISP seminar in Zhitomir as the "Sweet Couple of the Year for 2008." That is the translation from the Ukrainian language.

Above: I sweep Bonnie off her feet to the approval of Ukrainians at an ISP seminar in Zhitomir, in 2008.

Left: While Bonnie and I love to tour America's heartland in our Volvo and see what makes this country great, there is no place like home, not even the open road.

31

Roadside Assistance (1998)

Pling, plong!

A dashboard chime jerked me out of my trance. We were heading east on U.S. 36 in eastern Colorado. We were in our new 1998 Dodge Ram pickup with a slide-in Lance camper in the back. My wife was in the passenger seat reading Terry Anderson's *Den of Lions*.

"What was that?"

"I don't know."

The message center in the instrument cluster said, "Check gauges."

"Let's see . . . oil pressure, OK . . . temperature, OK . . . voltage, a bit low, but still in the normal range . . . fuel, OK."

We had just filled up.

At a loss for the cause, I pulled off beside the road and turned off the engine. Sometimes these lights will reset themselves after a restart. Not this time. The engine would not turn over. The three-quarter-ton Dodge Ram with a Cummins diesel is equipped with two batteries. Neither one of them had enough juice to give me a crank. I asked my wife to get the owner's manual out of the glove compartment, while I popped the hood. I was thinking that an old Volvo service representative like me should be able to figure something out, even on a Dodge.

My wife, who is seldom upset by mishaps or setbacks, decided to take a walk and inspect the local crop conditions, while I puzzled over the intricacies of the Dodge wiring system. I was still clueless when my wife returned and announced that help was on the way.

Pretty soon a young girl with a crew cut drove up in an aging midsize sedan. Never mind, though, with the help of an old set of jumper cables her 20-something Ford Fairmont energized my brand-new Dodge. But the warning light was still on.

We limped to the nearest filling station a few miles down the road in Idalia, Colorado. Not that I expected to find a mechanic on duty on a Sunday evening, but at least they had a phone. After all, Dodge offers 24-hour roadside assistance.

The young lady I reached at Dodge offered to provide a tow to the nearest dealer, who happened to be 60 miles in the wrong direction. She could not assure me that the dealer was equipped to handle my problem, so we decided to camp out and wait for Monday morning.

The gas station had been turned into a low-budget 7-Eleven. The lady on duty allowed us overnight parking next to their Dumpster. She also told us that Idalia is a community of about 90 people. The school draws students from a 60-mile radius, and her son was in a graduating class of 17 students. The town has two churches, no paved streets, and a community park and playground funded by the townspeople without tax subsidies. The little store she ran did not carry sugar, but she gave us half of her supply from the coffee stand, because we had forgotten to bring any.

Our camper was self-contained with its own electrical system. We would be OK for the night, even if the truck traffic on U.S. 36 did not allow for complete rest.

To my surprise, our truck started the following morning. Evidently, the batteries had recovered a little, but there was still no charge from the alternator. After some more checking, I discovered the main alternator fuse had blown. Dodge does supply a few extra fuses with every new truck. This 140-amp fuse was not one of them.

On the outskirts of town was a co-op store combined with a gas station. They offered everything from anhydrous ammonia to toilet seat seals and beef jerky, but no 140-amp fuses. They charged the batteries for half an hour, hoping that would be enough to get us to Atwood, Kansas, where there is a Dodge dealer.

The farmer, who fueled up his truck, while I was waiting around, was a Denver Bronco fan with a son in college on a football scholarship. "Maybe he can help me pay off the farm, if he turns pro." His crop of choice was pinto beans. His wife gave us some advice about how to prepare them.

The Dodge Boys, according to their red T-shirts, at Beamgard's in Atwood, tried to help. In fact, three of them took an interest in our predicament. In hearing their comments, I started to doubt whether they would be able to solve our problem.

"Man, that's a big camper you have got there."

"We don't stock these fuses."

"There sure are a lot of wires in these trucks these days."

Then they went to lunch, while my truck's batteries were being charged. They locked up the entire dealership, so when the rain rolled in, we took refuge in the camper and heated up a pizza. Even with a disabled truck, we would be able to survive, at least as long as the propane tank had something left in it.

After an hour on the charger, our rig started up again, and we headed south for Colby, Kansas, where Frontier Autoplex had indicated they stocked the fuse. Jimmy, one of the Dodge Boys, had called ahead on our behalf. Our problem had started in a community of 90 people. We had limped to Atwood, a town of a few thousand. Now I was hoping that Colby, population 6,000, would have enough resources to repair our truck. I don't know why, but Autoplex seemed to imply more resources than the Dodge Boys.

Jason Runnalls, the young service manager, was very forthcoming. There are two things a service customer doesn't want to hear: "Never seen that before." Or: "They all do that."

Jason didn't use either phrase, but he came close.

"Chrysler has got a bulletin out on that. We've got to replace the alternator, too."

So far, I was still reasonably relieved. At least they seemed to know what was going on.

Then he said, "We don't have an alternator. We can order one from Denver. It will be here some time tomorrow."

Spending the next 20 hours in an RV park next to Interstate 70 in flat Kansas was as if we were at anchor waiting for the wind to pick up. The following day Mr. Goodwrench (this was a combined Chrysler GM store) sacrificed his lunch hour to install the new alternator. Knowing that a failure rate of about 5 percent might generate a service bulletin, I figured I had a 95 percent chance of getting a good one this time.

Later, on the Interstate, with the new alternator revitalizing our batteries, I reflected on the episode. A total of 12 people had assisted us in various ways. Some had done it as part of their job. Others had done it out of simple, pure goodness. I was reminded of another time in another truck on the Capital Beltway in Washington, D.C. Our left rear tire exploded and disintegrated during Friday afternoon rush hour. The padlock for the spare was rusted shut. I was helpless, or so I thought. After less than a minute someone stopped, a strong young fellow with the right equipment, including a hydraulic jack. People helping strangers remains one of the strengths of this society. It is an old value that survives on the rural high plains and in hectic metropolitan traffic, and it is more dominant than road rage and car-jackings.

Sometimes road "angels" are young ladies in crew cuts. Sometimes the "angels" have huge biceps and carry hydraulic jacks.

32

Golf (1998)

My son was treating me to a round of golf for Father's Day. We were back in Virginia for a visit, and he had selected a fairly new golf course, which was still open to the public as it strived to build its membership roster. Since retirement, I had played my golf at public courses near our new home in Longmont, Colorado, and although it was not that long ago that we had left northern Virginia and the Capital area, I was not prepared for the contrast. As we got out of the car, an attendant nattily attired in a white shirt and a red vest approached us to assist us with our clubs. The clubhouse and the pro-shop were a mixture of English pub and country manor. Without thinking, I checked my slacks for wrinkles. My shoes could have used some polish, but it was too late to worry about that.

There was still a little time, before our scheduled tee time, so we went to the driving range to hit some balls. I looked around to acknowledge and greet the other golfers. No one paid any attention to us. I did not get the sense that they were that wrapped up in preparing for their round. Rather, it seemed, they were just focused on themselves. Most of them seemed to be upper 30s, upper-management types who get their haircuts by appointment only. Their golf apparel, that's right, not clothes, was strictly Nordstrom or expensive pro-shop stuff.

Being a person who is more comfortable in a Red Roof Inn than in a Red Carpet Lounge, I was amused thinking about my municipal home courses in Longmont, where most people walk the course, where blue jeans are acceptable attire and where the majority of the equipment people play with probably comes from Wal-Mart or K-mart.

My golfing buddies at Sunset or Twin Peaks in Longmont are predominantly retired folks, who are enjoying their rounds as they reflect on what they have accomplished in life. They are more likely to talk about their grandchildren than their next career move. They don't get bent out of shape by a bad lie or a lost ball. They will stop now and then and take in the breathtaking view of the Rockies and the Front Range. They are secure in who they are without a sense of self-importance. Partially this is probably a function of age, but I sense it is also a question of attitude.

The golf course there in the middle of northern Virginia horse country was undeniably a quality course, and I could not help but feel that one of the design criteria was to make an impression. In the sinister depths of my brain, I thought that was also the ambition of many of the golfers lined up with their carts at the first tee. Walking the course was out of the question. I felt out of place. The unpretentious approach to the game back home in Longmont had become my element.

Then I watched them tee off.

I realized that the game itself is a great equalizer. No matter how much money you have invested in equipment and apparel, you still have to address the ball squarely, take dead aim and sweep the grass. If you don't keep your head still and follow through, the slice will be as ugly at Raspberry Hills in Virginia as it is when I play Sunset in Colorado.

33

Flying (1999)

I used to enjoy flying. I even used to enjoy airline food. I have come to dislike flying, even though certain aspects of it can be rather amusing.

Consider that the FAA still insists people need to be taught how to buckle their seat belts. It is not very intricate, and it is standard equipment in cars. Flight attendants do their best to make the demonstration seem like a novel experience.

Some safety equipment cards show people in a life raft after an emergency water landing. It is wonderful how relaxed they look, lounging around in the life raft in the middle of some ocean. It looks more like some guided tour than an emergency situation.

Have you noticed how eager some people are to leave their seats after landing? The stewardesses have a tough job keeping everybody seated, until the captain has turned off the seat belt sign. The window seat passengers will pop up and stand doubled over under the overhead compartment for several minutes while the Jetway is being attached.

I think I am sometimes the only one checking my baggage. Huge garment bags and other suitcases are brought on board as carry-on luggage. Most of it is too heavy for someone to carry, which means they also bring on board luggage carts. So, there is seldom enough room for my coat in the overhead compartment. It comes out looking as if I have slept in it for a week.

I used to think I could master the ticket-price mystery. Not so. You are likely to find 30 or more different fares on the same flight. I read recently that United Airlines is installing a new super computer to maximize revenues. Watch out!

Why do people fly first-class? For twice the fare you get free drinks and wider seats. Clearly there is no price-to-value relationship. Perhaps the fact that you get to board at your leisure is the most compelling reason. That phrase is music to the ears of a weary business traveler.

When my daughters were growing up, they used to have me join them playing house. They would serve me tea and imaginary food on tiny little trays. I feel the same way about airline meals. The trays are small and awkward, space is limited and the food tastes vaguely make-believe. I have become sick from airline food on a couple of occasions. When I called to warn the airline about their potentially spoiled and dangerous salmon entrees, I was told to order a vegetarian meal the next time.

The reason I do not like flying is not so much about the hassles I have described. It is because I prefer to take the scenic route. Road trips reassure me that "my America," hometown America, still exists out there beyond the beltways and the Interstates.

Flying, then, presents a problem for me. You start out in a crowded airport in one congested city and end up in another. In this situation, at least on clear days, I do my best trying to spot "my America" from 30,000 feet. There are certain recognizable reassuring signs. I am not referring to the usual landmarks such as the Great Lakes, the Rockies or the Grand Canyon. What speaks to me more are grain elevators, irrigation circles and Little League baseball diamonds – signs of the heartland at work and at leisure. School buses are unmistakable signs that bring me back to Earth, at least figuratively. I wish I could feel as confident that we are as concerned about the values we teach in our schools as we are about the safety of the trip to school. Golf courses are plentiful, and they are often more serene than the cemeteries. Fast-food strips frequently seem to pollute otherwise pastoral scenes, and there are towns without McDonald's or Burger King. I do not think those folks are really deprived.

In airplanes, I am as impatient to "get there" as kids in the back seat of a car on a vacation trip. I can't wait to land.

PART SIX

Final Reflections

34

Some Sort of Accent

The apple doesn't fall far from the tree.
Old Swedish saying

People often tell me I have some sort of accent and ask where I am from. After telling them I am from Longmont, Colorado, I confess that I was born in Sweden. I am fairly sure that part of my accent is also influenced by my language-teaching background, making me rather pedantic about proper pronunciation. I don't mind those questions. Neither do I mind that there is a bit of a "Scandinavian accent" in my behavior.

While visiting Sweden on what felt like a bucket-list trip in 2012, I was somewhat startled by the passport control officer's question. "You gave up your Swedish citizenship?" After all, we were there to share my heritage with two of my grandchildren, and he made me feel a bit like a deserter.

I got over the incident rather quickly; I feel I have represented my heritage well even after pledging allegiance to my new country. Plus, our hosts were flying the American flag in their yard the entire time we stayed with them.

Yes, I am no longer a Swedish citizen, and I have pledged allegiance to my new country. That doesn't mean that I have renounced my heritage. Rather, I hope that at least some of my Scandinavian upbringing will be an asset to kids and grandkids, as well as to some of the people I interact with. Although I have lived over here longer than in Sweden, some of the old tendencies are still noticeable, even though my old countrymen think I am quite Americanized. That doesn't bother me at all.

I have sometimes bristled when my wife has referred to me over the years as a typical Northern European, but I have to admit that she has a point. This was made clear to me as I read a recent book about people from my part of the world. The author, Art Lee, is of Norwegian descent, and the book is called *Scandinavians Are Very Modest People But They Have Much To Be Modest About, Then*. As the author described his upbringing in the small town of Scandinavia, Wisconsin, I realized that we all – Swedes, Norwegians and Danes – do have lot in common. I was also reminded of Garrison Keillor's descriptions of the folks in Lake Wobegon. I am not exactly one of Keillor's Norwegian bachelor farmers, but I do admit to tendencies of being rather private and reserved.

I don't want to brag about Scandinavian modesty or humility, but focusing too much on your own abilities or achievements may not endear you to friends, neighbors or co-workers. This is not to say that initiative and individual achievements are to be discouraged or frowned upon.

Another personal observation is that Swedes are rather compliant people. As an example, the government, local or national, is usually referred to as the authorities. This may have something to do with the welfare state mentality. Personally, I detect very little of that tendency in my own feelings and comments about what goes on in Washington.

As mentioned earlier, as I was growing up, the Lutheran Church was the state church – in some sense just another government institution. Although my family belonged to one of the so-called Free Churches, I experienced this governmental influence in school, where Christianity was part of the curriculum. This was a good thing: Our morals and ethics were based on the Christian worldview but, at the same time, it didn't always lead to personal faith.

Sweden is known for its policy of neutrality through the years in world affairs. Don't jump to conclusions and look at both sides of the issue is definitely a Swedish tendency. This worked well for me in corporate life and allowed me to be the neutral mediator from time to time.

I have pledged and feel a strong allegiance to my adopted country; I also feel a lot of affinity to my Swedish background. Having "abjured all allegiance to foreign princes and potentates" doesn't mean I have to give up things like pickled herring and farmer's cheese along with other foods available at the closest IKEA store, which still warm my heart. Mind you, *lutfisk* is not part of that scenario. We still drive Volvos. I cheer for Sweden and the United States in the Olympics and other tournaments.

In retrospect, I recognize that all of us are influenced by our background and experiences – part cultural, part chosen, part faith – displayed in viewpoints, accents and behavior.

35

America's Leaders (1998)

We had stopped for the night in Smith Center in north-central Kansas. We were on one of our treks across the country heading back home to Colorado. We spent the night at the "Modern Aire Motel." It was perfectly adequate for a night's sleep, even though the term modern was no longer applicable. It probably had a total of 15 rooms, all with cinder-block interior walls. It was clean and tidy, and we did not mind at all that decor was not part of the ambiance. The rate was $44.06 including tax, and they were willing to put the ice block from our cooler in their freezer overnight. We slept well, and awoke refreshed and hungry.

"How about breakfast at one of the local restaurants, rather than dry cereal?"

"Great idea."

We discovered that two places were open for business early in the morning. Of course, we had risen rather early trying to get home at a decent time. We chose the "Lyon's Den" on the main business street that intersected Highway 36. The place was reasonably busy, although there were fewer pickup trucks parked outside than I expected. As I waited for my tall stack of pancakes with bacon, orange juice and coffee, I got out the road atlas.

"Somebody is going somewhere today I see."

I looked up and a young man in his 30s at the next table had turned around to speak to us. His enthusiasm and sparkling eyes attracted our attention. The fact that we were traveling from the East Coast interested him. He had recently visited Washington, D.C., and he gave us a rather detailed account of his trip. He had driven there with his wife, five children and a friend, camping along the way. We discovered that this was not the usual educational tourist trip to the nation's capital. He had gone there to "Stand in the Gap" with the Promise Keepers.

His name was Curtis, and he went on to share his faith in the Lord, his belief in strong families and his responsibility in teaching his children to believe in God, and the difference between right and wrong. He also spoke adoringly about his "awesome wife," who was home-schooling their children, while he ran a number of small businesses out of Portis, Kansas, 17 miles south on Highway 281. One of them was a Coca-Cola distributorship.

As I was saying grace before our meal, I glimpsed Curtis in the kitchen behind the cash register encouraging the staff with a smile and kind words. We left the restaurant nourished and revitalized in our spirits. When you look past the sunflowers and the corn, you find all sorts of examples of character and strength, examples of what has made this nation great, and nuggets of promise for the future. The leadership that this nation needs are fathers and mothers like Curtis and his wife. They are role models that will inspire the next generation.

36

The Good Times (1999)

It had been a rough winter emotionally with my mother's passing, which was the major reason I was back on the blood pressure medication. I had wrecked the car two weeks earlier, but now it was fixed, and the body shop had done a superior job. My mood was improving as I watched my wife drive away from the body shop with a big smile on her face.

The weatherman had promised a warm week ahead, so as I headed home in the truck, I stopped at a golf store to look around and pick up some balls. After looking at the vast selection of balls, I decided that the Wilson Staff Titanium Soft Spins would help me achieve my true potential. I was feeling pretty good as I turned onto Highway 287 in Fort Collins, heading south toward Longmont. As I tuned the radio to 104.3 FM, Classic Country, I was daydreaming about verdant fairways and perfectly groomed greens, where these balls would land with a soft thud and roll toward the cup. Thoughts about Volvo, my former employer, having been sold to Ford and my not being involved in the transition, unable to help preserve the soul of Volvo, started to fade into the background. Maybe retirement was OK, after all.

"Is the best of the free life behind us now and are the good times really over for good?"

Merle Haggard's unmistakable baritone suddenly surrounded me from the six-speaker stereo system of the truck. With the characteristic twang and nostalgia of country music, he lamented change and the loss of certain traditions and questioned some modern inventions such as microwave ovens.

When he mentioned Vietnam and intoned that Nixon lied to us all on TV, the 1998 Clinton impeachment mess flashed before my eyes, and we were bombing Serbia to boot. Gone were my thoughts about smooth swings, fairways and pars, when Haggard asked, "Are we rolling downhill like a snowball headed for Hell?"

I started to think, again, about the loss of our country's moral code. How big is this snowball? How fast is it rolling?

There is hope in the last verse of the song. Besides making a Ford and a Chevy that will last 10 years "like they should," we are told to "Stand up for the Flag and let's all ring the Liberty Bell." Agreeing with the final proclamation that the good times are not over for good, I turned down the volume as the ads and the announcer came on. It was time for reflection rather than commercial hype.

No, the good times aren't over, even for a retired guy with high blood pressure. My wife still loves me and she can cook, and she will, with or without a microwave. As I think about our grandchildren with their happy laughter and trusting eyes, I realize there is a role for each one of us.

Yes, we need to stand up for the Flag and the Liberty Bell. We also need to make sure future generations stand up for God and Country.

37

The County Fair (2002)

We took our two Colorado grandsons to the Boulder County Fair the other day.

We had charge of them for three days while our daughter was away on a trip. Jake is 5, and Luke is going on 3. They tend to take over the house while they stay with us. We keep a small basket of toys for them, and they also bring some of their own. Before long, you need to watch your step as you make your way across the great room. It is sort of like crossing a stream and trying to stay dry by stepping on the rocks. If you can find a safe spot on the carpet among train tracks, race cars, building blocks and assorted plastic farm animals, you can sometimes make it safely to the kitchen.

We thought it would be a good idea to give the home a rest and, at the same time, show them some real farm animals. We had taken them to the children's pool the previous day. It had been a good move. Fresh air and water play had resulted in a decent night's sleep for all of us. We were hoping the country fair would have a similar effect.

To be honest, it probably wasn't the farm animals that attracted the boys. Jake was old enough to remember the rides from a previous year. We also promised them cotton candy. Cotton candy is one of those county fair staples that bring back memories of bygone days. It is strange, but in all its non-nutritious fluffiness, it still reminds you somehow of traditional values and less complicated times. Ferris wheels give me a similar feeling of nostalgia. They move slowly and rock you gently without any surprises. Gazing down from the highest point, you get a sense of community as you watch others enjoying simple pleasures on a sunny afternoon.

At the age of 5 and just a few weeks before the start of kindergarten, Jake was anxious to try some of the most aggressive rides. Grandpa was reluctant, but in an unguarded moment of macho masculinity, I volunteered to go with him. I quickly realized that centrifugal forces work differently on a guy who is eligible for Social Security than they did in my younger days. I was fortunate that Jake did not qualify for the really rough rides.

There was an enclosure with all kinds of farm animals set aside for the kids. They were allowed to enter and mix with the roosters, chickens, donkeys, pigs, cows and ducks. Sometimes the kids and accompanying adults outnumbered the animals. These were animals that obviously had previous county fair experience. They seemed completely unperturbed by all the civilians from town. Some kids were reluctant to touch the animals, while others seemed ready to pick them up and take them home. It was all very safe and supervised by the folks who had brought the various critters and who showed remarkable patience with the people from town. The only hazard was really related to where you planted your feet as you made your way around.

In an adjacent area, some teenagers from the various farms proudly showed off their best specimens of sheep. These sheep had recently been shorn, and it was obvious that a lot of primping had taken place before this occasion. What struck me was the fact that the majority of the primping had been devoted to the sheep. They were exceedingly clean, if not to say polished. Obvious attention was also paid to how the sheep placed their hind legs. As the teenagers waited for the judge to decide who would get the first-place ribbon, they nervously kept repositioning the legs of the sheep. These were not your usual teenagers that you see hanging out in the malls, no designer jeans, nose rings, purple hair or pierced body parts. They were kids used to early morning farm chores in whose hands I will feel comfortable to place America's future. I am not just talking about them becoming national leaders on the political scene. They would be equally instrumental in determining the future of this nation as teachers in our schools. To me, these kids represent solid values, tradition, family and responsibility. That afternoon at the fair, they were for me a good antidote to the blank stares you encounter at the mall.

I will continue to take my grandsons to the fair. Along with the cotton candy and kettle corn that they want, I want them be exposed to these kids with their prized sheep.

38

One Nation, Under God (2003)

"Now, let's all rise for the Lord's Prayer and flag salute." This was the admonition that came to us over the speaker system at Montgomery Blair High School in Silver Spring, Maryland. The year was 1957 and, as an exchange student from Sweden, I was impressed by this demonstration of reverence and patriotism as students and their homeroom teachers bowed in prayer and also recited the Pledge of Allegiance in unison.

I experienced a lot as an exchange student and went back to my native country full of impressions and memories. My wife of almost 40 years is a living memory from that time, even though our love story really got started a few years later during a return visit. The year at Montgomery Blair, however, taught me a lot about uniting before the flag and reverence for our Creator. I do not recall any controversies surrounding this practice. There were no protests or petitions distracting the student body. Everyone, it seemed, was willing to participate.

My fellow students, for the most part, had parents or relatives who had been involved in service to their country during World War II, either in the armed forces or in some other capacity in the war effort on the home front. The Korean War was also fresh in everyone's memory. God and country united people in a natural way; most people still believed in absolutes, and parents and teachers were still authority figures. Perhaps there was one thing that really seemed to stir up some waves of protest. It was the fact that Elvis was drafted. That really got some of the teens riled up. The girls were particularly upset that he was forced to get a crew cut, although the King himself did not seem to mind.

The country stood for something – freedom, democracy and opportunity. A robust economy also made its contribution to an overall sense of pride and confidence. I felt privileged to witness all this, and I also had a sense that Sweden had been spared a lot during World War II, thanks to the fact that the Americans came to fight on the European continent to stem the tide of fascism. There was another thing that united the country in the '50s. Communism was the big new threat after the war. The Soviet bloc was an easily identifiable enemy and, in comparison to life behind the Iron Curtain, America was the shining example of democracy and freedom. People had little doubt in the fall of 1957 which system would prevail in the long run. Then, the first *Sputnik* was launched, and later Yuri Gagarin became the first man in space. All of a sudden, there was a comparison where the United States did not come out ahead. Was there something wrong with the system? Were we teaching enough science? Was there something wrong with our schools? To some degree, those questions are still being asked today, even though it is fair to say that after a fast start, the Soviets eventually lost the space race.

The country still stands for the same things it stood for in the '50s; in fact, what it has stood for since its inception. Today, however, we seem oddly divided over many of the things that this immigrant happens to think are what made this nation great. Anti-Americanism is strong, obviously, in the countries that hate us. Anti-Americanism is also doing quite well within the borders of this nation. How can this be, and what are some of the factors that contributed to this during that last 50 or so years? These questions have been asked before, and my answers are certainly not unique, but here is my take on it.

Bill Bennett, Chuck Colson and others have pointed to our institutions of higher learning, where Marxism in new disguises seems to flourish. Communism has turned out to be a bankrupt system in Eastern Europe and the former Soviet Union, but Marxist philosophies have not yet retreated from our universities. Unless we stem this tide, this will have a devastating impact on generations of young people.

Vietnam and Woodstock in the '60s and Watergate in the '70s had a divisive and corrosive influence. A lot of informed commentary has been written on these subjects, and I have nothing new to add to the debate. However, it is sometimes hard to determine what is cause and what is effect. Watergate certainly has contributed to a cynical attitude and distrust for our government, but in one sense it is just as much a symptom of trying to navigate without a moral compass. In today's relativistic postmodern America, freedom of choice seems to be the most important right to many. To suggest that certain behaviors are destructive to the individual and to society is considered bigotry. In recent years, we have witnessed immorality, dishonesty and greed in the highest places. Certainly we should guard our liberties, but that does not mean we need to condone everything.

There are those who hold up the Constitution as some sort of guarantee given to us by the Founding Fathers allowing us to behave as we choose without regard to the consequences for society. They would do well to consider what some of these same Founding Fathers said about morality and religion. Bill Bennett gives several examples in his book *The De-valuing of America.*

In George Washington's Farewell Address, we find, "Of all the dispositions and habits which lead to political prosperity, religion and morality are indispensable supports. . . . And let us with caution indulge the supposition that morality can be maintained without religion." John Adams makes this sobering observation, "Our Constitution was made only for a moral and religious people. It is wholly inadequate to the government of any other."

It is a good sign that the debate over the Pledge of Allegiance and the phrase "one nation, under God" waned as quickly as it did.

In spite of what is reflected in the media, where the postmodern intellectual elite have a disproportionate share of voice, Americans as a whole are closer to the sentiments of the Founding Fathers. Elite society often fails to take into account the part of America normally flown over between our two coasts. The voice from the heartland was heard loudly in this debate. To its credit, the political leadership also rose to the occasion. We cannot, however, become complacent. There are signs of a not-so-gradual shift away from moral absolutes. George Barna reports that this is happening even among Christians. This is alarming, and we need to stem the tide. Even though attitudes of the "Baby Boomers" are influencing the current cultural debate, one day they will turn this country over to what some have called "the pierced generation." They will one day lead, but they will be guided by the values we have left them as our legacy. We must not fail them.

39

My Wish List

- A clean windshield and a full tank of gas.
- A drive that goes straight down the fairway.
- The Broncos on Monday Night Football.
- The congregation singing, "How Great Thou Art."
- A sunset over the Rockies.
- A patio facing west.
- Kathy Mattea live, singing, "Mary, Did You Know?"
- Grandchildren who love the Lord.
- A steady breeze on the Chesapeake Bay.
- A close-hauled run to Thomas Point Light.
- A smiling grandchild.
- A phone call from an old staff member.
- A round in the 80s.
- A quiet campsite.
- One nation, under God.
- A groomed cross-country trail.
- A dogleg left.
- A person, not voice mail, at the other end.
- Low humidity.
- Low cholesterol.
- Better weed control.
- To make a difference.

- Accuracy in media.
- A smooth idle.
- Fewer barnacles.
- Respect for the truth.

40

I Still Remember

- Going with Grandma Gerda when she was a cleaning lady at the local school and I was allowed to write with real chalk on the blackboard.
- Then there was the amazing time when colored chalk was available.
- A field trip into town to see a new invention called television.
- When nobody in our neighborhood except for the local grocer had a car.
- When five families on our block shared a push lawnmower.
- Trying to bike on wet cobblestone streets.
- Steam engine train rides to summer camp.
- Street crews with horses and carts rather than trucks to carry tools and material.
- When Sweden got a second TV channel.
- Trucks, buses and cars running on producer gas by burning wood and charcoal.
- Food-rationing coupons during WWII.
- Going with my folks into the woods to pick mushrooms and blueberries to supplement our food supply.
- A local seamstress making my best Sunday clothes, salvaging parts from Dad's suits and uniforms.

.

Appendix

After a few guest opinions submitted to our local paper, the *Longmont TIMES-CALL*, had been published, the managing editor asked me to write a regular monthly column. The first one appeared in February of 2006, and I have enjoyed the opportunity to express my views on a variety of subjects ever since. Local readers have provided feedback of both the positive and negative kind. Recently, I asked the editor, if these contributions could be more sporadic. He was kind enough to allow me to continue at a pace that suits my current situation in life.

I have selected a few of these columns for this part of the book, and it is my hope that they will further illustrate my beliefs and values. Yes, there is a certain amount of criticism regarding some current trends in the nation, but I have tried to balance that by affirming what is good about the country that accepted me as a citizen.

Citizenship test nothing compared to sacrifices

The federal government has launched an effort to revamp the citizenship exam. The Associated Press reported recently that candidates for citizenship can opt for a new version of the test on a voluntary basis. If they don't pass, they can take the regular test that has been in use for many years. This is a pilot program taking place in 10 cities nationwide this year.

The new test represents an effort to move from memorization to concepts and is designed make the applicants come up with thoughtful answers. To pass, you have to answer six out of 10 questions correctly.

Following the pilot program, the government will spend a year studying the results and fine-tuning the process and the questions. The project to revise the test will cost an estimated $6.5 million.

It will be interesting to see how many applicants will opt for the new test. I am not sure what my choice would have been years ago when I applied for citizenship, but the entire process came to mind as I read about the new approach. It is worth noting that the test is only a minor part of the naturalization process, which is rather lengthy and requires a lot of documentation.

Although I appreciate the need for background checks, I do confess that I was irritated by some of the minutiae of the application. At the same time, I was surprised that we evidently assume that potential terrorists or drug dealers would answer these background questions truthfully.

When it was all over and we were ready for the naturalization ceremony, all the irritation was gone. I proudly, and with a lot of emotion, took the Oath of Allegiance along with hundreds of others, who had chosen this country as their new home. In doing so, we joined millions of immigrants from all over the world who had come to these shores to build a better future.

The somewhat archaic language of the oath, where I promised to "abjure all allegiance and fidelity to any foreign, prince, potentate, state or sovereignty," added to the solemnity of the occasion. So, actually, did the presence of representatives from the Daughters of the American Revolution.

In taking the oath, new citizens make certain promises which are in some aspects similar to what is required of people volunteering for military service. This is something all of us must take seriously. I was in total agreement with the final phrase in the oath: "and [that] I take this obligation freely without any mental reservation or purpose of evasion; so help me God."

Once you are approved as citizen, you don't have to jump through any hoops to retain your status. The various documents that allow me to fish, drive and travel abroad have expiration dates, but my naturalization papers are for life. That's why it is important that we get it right the first time.

I am grateful to a nation that has welcomed me as a citizen. It is my intent to live up to all the obligations of citizenship and the principles I swore to uphold. We should all be grateful to the founders, whether we are Americans by naturalization or by birth. We are reaping the benefits of their dedication and foresight. Some of them had to pay a great personal price implied in the words "we mutually pledge to each other our Lives, our Fortunes, and our Sacred Honor."

The Founding Fathers risked a lot and some did indeed lose their fortunes, while others had to leave their homes. (The book *Our Sacred Honor* by William J. Bennett gives a moving account of all this, quoting from their personal letters and speeches.)

Answering six out of 10 questions correctly pales in comparison.

February 26, 2007

★ ★ ★

Unity in the U.S. does not imply uniformity

"Now you can call yourselves Americans." Those words meant a lot. The government official, who administered the ceremony, when I became a U.S. citizen, went on to say something that was perhaps just as meaningful. He told us that we had an obligation to share our background and the best of the customs and traditions of the country of our birth with our children, grandchildren and the people in our communities.

He also talked about how America as a nation is richer, stronger, more welcoming and understanding because of the successful blend of nationalities and backgrounds represented across this land. More

149

than a million of my countrymen had preceded me as immigrants, and I wasn't sure what my particular contribution might be in this regard.

I realized, of course, that several Swedes have achieved household-name status. Carl Sandburg and Charles Lindbergh come to mind. Eric Wickman may not be all that familiar to most people, but his company, Greyhound, has served this nation well. Walgreens, with an ever-increasing presence, is another example. Most Swedish immigrants, however, have had a more anonymous impact on the fabric of American life as will certainly be true in my case. That is OK, so long as it is positive.

Comments of a similar nature can be made about immigrants from around the globe. Our nation has been characterized by immigration. Even our common language has come here from another country, and just like our culture, it is richer and more colorful, thanks to adopting words from other languages. What's your *shtick*? Who is your *ombudsman*? Have another *hors d'oeuvre*.

The same can be said about the food we enjoy. The Wayside Inn in Berthoud used to offer a Swedish Christmas brunch, and in Longmont we can enjoy a variety of restaurants with international cuisine. Countries such as China, Japan, Mexico, Italy and even Thailand are represented. Of course, living here in ranch country, I consider it a civic duty to eat a good steak now and then. Nothing satisfies like beef.

As we enjoy a wonderful blend of customs and traditions from around the world, let's remember that the assimilation must not stop. It has been the key to the success of this melting pot. The process has produced a country where resourcefulness, opportunity, freedom of choice and individual responsibility have yielded extraordinary results.

Certainly there are those, both at home and abroad, who question the soundness of our society. I suspect that the criticism abroad is partially rooted in a certain amount of envy. The United States continues to be a destination of choice. Sometimes the criticism seems louder internally, and there is no denying that we need to recognize certain blemishes and problems.

There is no need, however, to throw up our hands in despair. History and tradition suggest that we can solve our problems as long as we face the facts and work together. Sometimes partisanship gets in the way. At other times, personal ambition seems to trump the common good.

We need to recognize that the government has a role, but public policy solutions are not the only way to go. It is often quicker and cheaper when people unite around a common cause. Individual initiative can work wonders. The cradle-to-the-grave mentality so common in Europe, with its tendency to delegate everything to the government, has shown signs of weakness for several decades.

So let's recognize and celebrate what has made this country great and given us a unique role in the world. Let's remind ourselves that unity does not imply uniformity, and that patriotism includes an aspect of striving for common goals for the public good.

April 26, 2007

* * *

Measuring a healthy culture beyond the Cold War

It was early October 1957, and my American adventure had just begun. I was in my second month as an exchange student from Sweden at Montgomery Blair High School in Silver Spring, Maryland.

My first few weeks in the States had been somewhat overwhelming – a sharp contrast to what I was used to. The fact that the high school parking lot was jammed with cars belonging to the students indicated resources and a standard of living unheard of in my own country. Beyond that, however, I had experienced an attitude of friendliness and openness that took some getting used to for a somewhat reserved northern European. Then there was this contagious optimism along with a can-do attitude that seemed so natural among students and adults alike.

Those were heady days when Ford invited you to "try the Thunderbird magic" and proclaimed the Fairlane to be "poetry on wheels." The U.S. auto industry seemed invincible, the V8s reigned supreme, and gas was 29 cents per gallon. Elvis had not yet been drafted. America was rocking.

Then, suddenly, there was the surprising announcement that the Soviets had launched their *Sputnik* satellite. This led to a lot of questioning and second-guessing. "Are they that good?" "Is there something wrong with our educational system?"

Tom Wolfe in the book *The Right Stuff* refers to John McCormack of the House of Representatives saying that the United States faced "national extinction" if it did not overtake the Soviets in the space race. The book also describes the space race as an old-fashioned, "single combat" scenario with the astronauts representing the nation.

It turns out that America was ready to compete. *Explorer I* was launched four months later, and in just over a decade, the Apollo program put a man on the moon.

Although the fears may have been overstated, the fact remains that competing with the Soviets in space and elsewhere during the Cold War era kept us sharp and focused. With the Soviets no longer serving as a logical comparison, we have to look elsewhere to calibrate our progress and the health of our culture.

Events and cultural trends in the 1960s were not so positive. The wounds of Vietnam have taken a long time to heal and still surface from time to time. Riots and what seemed to be an exploding drug culture are other examples. The Kennedys and King assassinations again raised some doubts. "Where are we heading?" "Are things spinning out of control?"

Early in the 21st century, we would do well to remember that a strong economy and military might are not the only measures of success.

Civil harmony, morality and virtue must be the basis for a healthy culture.

October 22, 2007

★ ★ ★

Memorable statements from five decades of presidents

Different things come to mind when I think of the various U.S. presidents who have served during my lifetime. Dwight Eisenhower was one of the earliest. Yes, I am old enough for him not to be the first one. He occupies a special place in my memory since he took time to speak to several hundred exchange students, as we had gathered on the White House lawn back in 1958.

As I recall the ones who have followed him, it is often things they have said in office or while campaigning for office that are etched in my memory.

Kennedy's admonition, "Ask not what your country can do for you – ask what you can do for your country," is as compelling today as it was in 1961. Kennedy's oratory, debating skills and agility in press conferences have never been equaled by any one of his followers. His New England accent made him stand out even more.

Ronald Reagan's speech on June 12, 1987, at the Brandenburg Gate in Berlin did not receive massive press coverage at the time. One statement stood out, "Mr. Gorbachev, tear down this wall." The Communist news agency Tass accused Reagan of war-mongering, but it took only a little over two years before dismantling operations began. The Cold War was coming to a close.

Other presidents have sometimes had a tough time living up to or even living down some things they have said. "Read my lips: no new taxes" was a clever phrase in George H.W. Bush's acceptance speech at the 1988 Republican National Convention.

Boy, did that come back to haunt him, when he had to compromise with Congress during his first term and raise several taxes to deal with the deficit at the time.

I will be discreet and not go into detail about what I remember from Bill Clinton's time in office, but it has to do with the definition of a common verb.

George W. Bush is often ridiculed for his slips of the tongue. One of my favorites is, "They misunderestimated me." Sometimes I wonder if what we affectionately refer to as Bushisms really were slips of the tongue. Perhaps it was just a technique to make sure we paid attention.

What about the current president? Is there one statement that stands out? "We are five days away from fundamentally transforming the United States of America" is a phrase that certainly deserves notice. It was a proclamation that startled me. Well into his first term, I must admit that he has not forgotten his promise. Our government is reaching further into our individual lives as well as commerce. Polls indicate that everyone is not pleased.

I am comforted by the fact that to radically transform America, you must first radically transform Americans. That is something no president can or should do.

August 23, 2010

★ ★ ★

Truths of the past are no longer self-evident

It occurs to me that the Dutch and the Chinese have something in common. During the Revolutionary War, the Dutch extended several loans, often brokered by John Adams, to finance the fight against England. This was critical to the success of the war and the birth of this nation.

As we are all aware, China is now holding a large portion of our national debt. We can take little comfort in the fact that this is not the first time we have run a deficit. The reasons for deficit spending are vastly different now. The nation's founding principles, which led to the fight for independence, were based on certain self-evident truths. People were willing to fight for these principles, and also pledge their lives fortunes and sacred honor.

Listening to the current debate about the proposed budget and the deficit, it is clear that things are a lot less self-evident these days. Yes, they all say we can't afford to continue to spend what we don't have. Beyond that there is little agreement.

There were heated debates even in the early days in the Continental Congress and later between Federalists and Republicans, on how to proceed, but the founding principles still retained some freshness, and as a result, sound decisions were made.

This immigrant finds the thoughts and wisdom contained in the historical documents and letters very enlightening.

In his first inaugural address, Thomas Jefferson laid out what he considered the essential principles of government. Noteworthy in the context of our current economic situation is his mention of "economy in public expense" in the same sentence as "sacred preservation of the public faith." In a previous paragraph, he envisioned a wise and frugal government, "which shall restrain men from injuring one another, shall leave them otherwise free to regulate their own pursuits of industry and improvement."

The balance between too much and too little government involvement has been debated for centuries. This is illustrated by the fact that the often quoted statement, "That government is best which governs least," has been attributed to both Jefferson and Paine, but may have originated with Thoreau.

Liberty, though, puts its own burdens on the people. In a speech at the Virginia ratifying congress, James Madison warned that to suppose that any form of government could secure liberty or happiness without any virtue in the people would be futile.

What strikes me in looking through some of the writings and proclamations from the early days of this country are the frequent references to Divine providence, the Almighty and the Supreme Judge of the world. Indeed, the Declaration of Independence stating that "all men are created equal, that they are endowed by their Creator with certain unalienable Rights" might even be termed politically incorrect in today's environment.

I am glad that thought did not cross the minds of the Founding Fathers.

February 28, 2011

★ ★ ★

Bridge, rest stop, role model

I don't recall who it was, but someone once reflected on his potential legacy saying that he would rather have a bridge bearing his name than a rest stop along the New Jersey Turnpike.

Having driven up and down that toll road more times than I care to count, I can relate to the sentiment. The George Washington Bridge, which spans the Hudson River close to the north end of the turnpike, connects Manhattan with New Jersey, is esthetically inspiring and can handle a lot of traffic efficiently.

The turnpike has a dozen rest areas, all of them very similar to each other. They are nice enough and provide the necessary amenities: You can fill the gas tank, have a bite to eat and take care of other personal needs. However, inspiring is not a word that comes to mind as you pull off the highway.

I am not sure how honored the people, whose names were used to name the areas, would feel, if they were aware of their distinction. Vince Lombardi is there along with Grover Cleveland and Thomas Edison. James Fenimore Cooper and Walt Whitman represent literary history. The list goes on.

So, some or our presidents get airports or aircraft carriers named after them, while others have to settle for a rest area along a busy toll road or perhaps an avenue in a small town.

We also have the folks who have products named after them. That's good, at least if the product is successful, but, for example, the Ford Edsel, introduced in September of 1957, was a failure and did not honor the memory of Henry Ford's son. He had led the company successfully until his death in 1943, and also had given generously to various causes, but rather than the intended tribute, the name Edsel is associated with failure.

Some products are so successful and lasting that the name turns into a normal noun and the originator is all but forgotten. When talking about diesel engines and diesel fuel, few of us think about Rudolf Diesel, but his invention, which he patented in 1898, has had a huge impact on the trucking and railroad industry.

Most of us do not have to worry whether we will get a bridge or a rest stop named after us. I certainly admire people like Washington and Edison, but it occurs to me that the people who have had the most impact on my own life and values are not the sort who are immortalized with a monument or have their name on a bridge, even a small one. My role models were parents, bosses, co-workers and friends. We can all have an impact, even if we are not presidents or celebrities.

January 30, 2012

* * *

Your 'check body' light is lit

Recently, I have been perplexed by a temperamental "check engine" light in my car. I drive a Volvo, and yes, even a product of "superb Swedish engineering" (an old tagline from Volvo ads in the 1950s) can play tricks on you. My Volvo is, as are all newer cars, subject to this federally mandated warning light resulting from the Clean Air Act.

What is perplexing is the fact that the problem comes and goes. Even when the light is on, the car runs fine, and performance and fuel mileage are not affected. It is, as it were, a symptom-free condition and probably not terminal, to use language from the medical field. The owner's manual still suggests that you consult a specialist, in this case a Volvo retailer, as soon as possible.

"Check engine" is a bit of a misnomer, since the second- generation onboard diagnostic system, referred to as OBD II, monitors not only the engine and emissions, but also the transmission and the electrical system.

Not wanting to be nonchalant about the federal mandate, I took the car to my friendly dealer. After the test procedure, which produced a seven-page printout of the various DTCs (diagnostic trouble codes), I was assured that there was no need for any repairs at this time. Evidently, there is occasionally a slight drop in voltage to a certain component. This news pleased me, of course. In addition, there was no "co-pay" at this time.

I guess we should be grateful for these sophisticated diagnostic procedures, but I sometimes miss the good old days. My 1959 Volvo had twin SU carburetors. They were kind of tricky to adjust, but there was something special about working on them in the driveway with the help of a friend using simple tools.

Big brother is watching these days, and the check engine light is the car's "conscience," meant to keep us in line and making sure we don't pollute. We also get a lot of information we don't need. I wonder if it is really necessary to keep track of hundreds of various nuances in a car's performance. Then again, I am just a shade tree mechanic, at best.

Of course, it may come in handy when we buy a used car. Running an OBD test might let you know there are no "pre-existing conditions."

You can probably tell that the constant chatter about a government healthcare program has influenced my vocabulary. Indeed, perhaps what we need is an IBD, or in body diagnostic system. I can imagine a microchip implanted in the brain keeping track of how my body performs. Why did my heart skip a beat? What was the reason for that coughing spell? A message on my cell phone would let me know what is going on and upload the data to the appropriate physician. I am not sure it would add to my peace of mind, or lower healthcare costs, if it were made a federal mandate.

October 29, 2012

* * *

Choices: Exit or do not enter

Disney World in Florida is quite an attraction for both young and old. We have been there a few times with our kids, when they were younger; with my folks, when they were visiting from Sweden; and also in corporate settings.

Being of Scandinavian ancestry, I personally enjoyed the Norway pavilion at the Epcot Center, although I sort of wished they had tried to give you a feeling of Sweden instead; just nostalgia you understand. Later, while walking through Epcot's version of Morocco, I was fascinated by how real it all seemed. In no time I felt transported to this interesting country in North Africa. Suddenly, I was brought back to reality. Walking through a narrow alley I spotted a sign: "Emergency Exit." I thought, "I guess we are not in Morocco anymore."

A number of years later, my wife and I attended a corporate meeting near Malaga, Spain. Some of our retail partners were being rewarded for excellent performance. The fact that the Ryder Cup was being played at nearby Valderama was no coincidence.

One day we invited some of the dealers for a trip across Gibraltar to Tangier, Morocco. It was an interesting trip, but after a while I had had enough of dark alleys, haggling with street merchants and young men volunteering to be your guide for a day in exchange for a few dollars. But alas, there was no emergency exit. This was reality, not some theme park in Florida.

I have to admit there are occasions in real life when an emergency exit would be real nice. We have all encountered them.

I remember checking into a hotel once and getting the wrong room assignment, thus ending up walking into a room that was already occupied. "Oops, let me get out of here, quickly."

Once after a corporate gathering at headquarters in Sweden, a three-hour layover in Amsterdam turned into an overnight. "Please, where is the emergency exit? My team needs me back in the States." Deep down I knew, of course, that another day with the boss overseas was perhaps not really bad news for some of them, but rather an opportunity to show their independence.

On a more serious note, perhaps we are listening to a doctor giving us a certain diagnosis and come to realize that we are trapped in a deteriorating body, which does not function the way it used to. Good prescription medicine can only do so much, if there is no known cure.

There are no easy emergency exits in real life. That's when the support of friends and family is so important. For a person of faith, though, the old saying "This too shall pass" does apply. The best is yet to come.

I know, Ted Turner of CNN fame, once proclaimed that "Christianity is a religion for losers." Others, famous or not so famous, have expressed similar convictions. A lot of people these days seem to have a sense of discomfort with Christianity. Indeed, atheists throughout history have gone to great lengths to proclaim that there is no God. It reminds me of Irina Ratushinskaya, a Soviet author from the city of Odessa. During her time in the Communist school system with its teachings of atheism, she found it odd that there was such a fuss by the atheists running the country about someone they said did not exist anyway.

We all have to make a choice whether to believe in God or not, but we must acknowledge that, if he exists, he is who he is. Unbelief won't make him go away. He is who he is, no matter how we define him. He is who he is, no matter how some of his followers behave; we are all a work in progress.

April 30, 2013

* * *

Of world events and personal paths

On November 22, 1963, I had spent my lunch hour walking around the Battery Park area at the southern tip of Manhattan. My normal routine was to try to get some fresh air before returning to my desk at the main office of the Chase Manhattan Bank near Wall Street. I was expecting to crunch numbers for the remainder of the day.

The atmosphere in the office had never been very boisterous, but this day I found it unusually somber. Several of my co-workers had heard on the news that the President had been shot. It wasn't long before we found out that he had died. I don't believe we got much work done that afternoon.

People were also unusually quiet on the subway during the ride back to my small apartment on 74th Street; many were staring at dramatic pictures in the evening papers. It was hard for me to grasp what had taken place. A short time earlier, I had seen John F. Kennedy's motorcade in New York City. He had looked relaxed and vigorous waiving to the public from his open limo. Now he was dead. What was going to happen? Was the country ever going to be the same?

Later that evening, the details of the event and its immediate aftermath became clear to me, as they were related by Walter Cronkite of CBS News in his calm and almost fatherly voice. This is long before we had 24-hour cable news channels.

Although we lived in Europe later in the '60s and early '70s, I still followed closely what was going on in the country I had first experienced when Eisenhower was president. From across the ocean, we heard about riots and protests and an emerging counterculture movement with the hippies and the Woodstock festival. Some commentators have talked about the country losing its innocence when the "Camelot Presidency" – a term first used by Mrs. Kennedy – ended.

Shortly after we returned to the States, President Nixon resigned. Yes, America was not quite what I was used to, but we shouldn't ignore some positives. The landmark Civil Rights Acts of the '60s stand out in my mind.

Whatever we think about what is going on in our country today, the United States can still be an example to the rest of the world, as long as we focus on what unites us rather than on our differences. We cannot continue to let a certain aisle in the Capitol divide us as a nation.

Depending on our age, many of us remember other historical moments or watershed events. I was just a kid when WWII ended, but I will never forget when Dad told me there was peace, which was largely due to the U.S. having joined the effort to defeat Hitler. I also recall when the Russians launched their *Sputnik*, which led to the space race and eventually the moon landing.

World events may of course change nations, but they can also influence us as individuals. As I look back, though, I know that my own personal decisions have shaped my life more than world events. I never imagined how my decision to apply for a scholarship to attend high school in this country would impact the rest of my life. Whatever plans I had back then were not close to what has happened: a different career, marrying my American sweetheart, a new citizenship, retired life in Colorado, just to mention some of the excitement.

Of course, there have been some challenges, but one thing has remained since my early teen years – my trust on a personal level in the God of the Bible. I am reminded of the verse, Proverbs 16:9: "In his heart the man plans his course, but the Lord determines his steps."

November 25, 2013

★ ★ ★

In a year of battles, less concern about the 'war on Christmas'

In view of all the conflicts both at home and abroad grabbing our attention and tugging at our heart strings, I had expected that we would have been spared the annual December skirmishes. I am talking about the war on Christmas. I guess that was too much to ask.

Here is one example. This year's billboard by American Atheists shows a young girl next to her message to Santa, "Dear Santa, all I want for Christmas is to skip church! I am too old for fairy tales." The organization claims that the campaign is aimed at "closet atheists who are pressured to observe religious traditions during the holidays." It is hard for me to guess at the age of the little girl, and the smile on her face makes me wonder if she even knew how the picture would be used.

Anyway, she is too old for fairy tales but evidently young enough to count on Santa's help. I am not sure what age that would be. Also, she is apparently not aware that the word Christmas is taboo among atheists; that's assuming she penned the message on her own. Of course the word "holiday," which is preferred by many of those who fight Christmas, makes little sense either since they don't regard the season as holy.

So how crowded are the closets where the pressured atheists hide? And how many atheists are there out in the open? I have looked at various polling data, but it is hard to arrive at a definite conclusion. For example, one survey indicated that 14 percent of those who call themselves atheists also say that they believe in God or a universal being. I did not come across any data showing how many of them believe in Santa. One poll conducted by Pew Research had the number of atheists at 1.8 percent, but then again there were some who evidently answered "don't know" when asked about their religious beliefs. Polls can be rather confusing at times.

I used to get quite riled up about the fight over Christmas, but as I was writing this, I realized how my focus is less and less on what is allowed to be displayed at different venues. That is just dealing with symptoms rather than fundamentals. I can trace my change in attitude to what is going on in the world and what has happened to our family during the past year.

We all know there are many trouble spots around the globe, and there is no need to list them all. Personally, the ongoing conflict in Ukraine has affected me quite a bit. For years, I have had the privilege to work with many teachers at various conferences in that country on the issue of character education. As they have shared their concerns about their country, I have come to realize how blessed we are over here in spite of the yearly arguments about the upcoming holiday.

On a personal level, what has happened during this year in our family has also influenced my perspective. In January, our son's family lost an eagerly awaited baby son, who did not survive an emergency C-section. This will also be the first Christmas without our beloved oldest daughter who passed away in August. She had dealt with serious health issues for a number of years, but her death was still a shock to the entire family. Parents outliving their children is not the expected sequence of events. I am sure many of my readers can relate to that. Though there will always be an empty place during family gatherings, we know her suffering is over, and based on her Christian faith and ours, it is our conviction that we will see her again. In the meantime, we will enjoy the precious memories.

Many, probably most of you, will agree with our family perspective; a few will call it wishful thinking based on fairy tales. Either way, I wish you all a Merry Christmas.

December 22, 2014

Printed in the United States
By Bookmasters